PYTHON PROGRAMMING

Comprehensive Beginners Guide to Learn Python Programming from A-Z

TABLE OF CONTENTS

Introduction

Developed by Guido van Rossum, Python is a very robust and straightforward program language to use for your programming project. It was initially introduced into the market in 1991. Python enables people to note minimal mission swiftly.

Advantages of Using Python

1) Python Is Easy to Use

The primary objective of any Python programming language is to traverse the distance between the programmer's mind and that of the PC. Some of the most known languages include C, Java, C++, and C#, are referred to be high-level languages, this implies that they are always nearer to the human language as compared to machine language. Python language is very close to the English language as compared to any other language, with its coherent and simple regulations. Developing Python programming is very direct that it has been referred to as programming at the speed of thought.

The ease application Python renders into productivity for executive programmers. Python programs are precise and haul minimal time to develop as compared to any other programs that are noted in other known languages. It is argued that Python programs are 3 to 5 times precise as contrasted other programs like Java, and generally 5 to 10 times brief as compared to C++ programs. Many Python programmers suggest there is a lot of proof to illustrate how a single Python programmer could complete in just two months other programs like C++ can take more than two years.

2) *Python Is Robust*

Python language contains all the strength a person could anticipate from a digital programming language. After a careful interpretation of this book at the end, you will be in a position to note programs that utilizes process file, GUI, and include multimedia components such as the sound, graphics, and the animation.

The powerfulness of Python is adequate to captivate many programmers internationally, and companies like Google, Microsoft, NASA, among others. In addition, it is applied as a piece of equipment by professional game programmers all around the world. Companies like Infogrames and others to publish their games to include Python.

3) *Python Is Object-Oriented*

If for instance, you have come across anything associated with Python programming, then you must have more likely hard the terminology of object-oriented programming (OOP). This topic is typically a hot one, and OOP contains three main letters that each programmer takes into consideration on their resume. The object focused programming generally is a take in the means in which programmers ponder in dealing with issues related to computers. It entails a mechanical means illustrating data and activities in a program. Python programs are also not the only mean to note programs, but when relating to extensive programs, we can say yes, it is the only way to go.

Languages such as Python, C#, and Java, are mostly object-oriented. But Python is the most preferred one because it performs better. In other language programs such as the C# and Java, the object-oriented programming is compulsory. This results in short programs becoming complicated and thus would need unnecessarily complex, and requires a bunch of clarification before a brand new programmer could perform anything significant. With Python, the approach taken is always very different; it applies the model and considers it optional. A person who uses Python has all of the OOP's strengths on their disposal, but he/she may refer to it when it is needed. Do you have a brief program that does not need the Object-Oriented Programming? Be comfortable, since we have an extended plan with a group of programmers that require OOP. I think that that can work too because Python gives people power and flexibility to do various activities.

4) *Python Runs Everywhere*

From a Palm to a Cray Python operates everything. Nevertheless, even though you may not have a supercomputer in your house, we assure you that possible to operate Python on Windows, Macintosh®, DOS, or Linux engines. This is just at the top of the chart; Python may also practically operate on each existing functioning system.

One of the components of Python programs is that it is also an independent platform, to signify that irrespective of their running/operating system that an individual can apply to develop his or her program, actually Python program can operate on any computer device that has Python in its network. So if we write a game on our computer, we can basically e-mail a copy to our pals who operate a Linux or to our aunt who poses a Mac and the project will function this would imply that as long as our pal and aunt obtain the Python program on their computers they can operate their programs.

5) *Python Has a Strong Community*

Many individuals apply Python in their daily tasks, and indeed the society is developing day by day. Indeed the dealing at the *comp.lang.Python* newsgroup, where all sorts of individuals join to learn about Python, doubles almost every two years.

Most programming languages obtain a determined newsgroup. Besides this Python contain other things known as the Python Tutor mailing chart, a more casual mean for commencing programmers to enquire those original questions. Even though the list is identified as Tutor, anyone can reply questions.

The general components shared by Python communities are that they appear to be open and friendly, although other Python communities are determined in different areas. That would only sound convincing because Python language is so approachable for beginners.

6) *Python Is a "Glue" Language*

The Python language can be blended with other languages like Java, C, and C++ since it would imply that that the programs could get the advantage of work which is already performed in another language while applying Python. Besides, it means that you may grip the powers of other languages, like the additional speed that C or C++ can provide, while still relish the ease of growth that is attributed to Python programming

7) *Python Is Free and Open Source*

Any individual can install Python program on their PCs without paying anything since Python is free. But if you register for Python license, you would be able to do a little more than installing the Python. One of them would be: being able to copy or redefine Python. With this, you can even resell Python if you opt to. Welcoming such free-source paradigms like this is a section of what creates Python well known and successful.

Chapter One

Python Basics

Programming typically refers to the process of acquiring a PC to perform specific task/activities. The definition is not one of the most complex ones; it is a precise one, indeed. By studying Python, you will be in a position to develop a program, whether the program can be an easy game, a minimal utility, or a business product, with all characterized GUI, a graphical user interface. It will appear that it belongs to a person like the program a person has created, and will perform what it has been instructed by you. Programming is regarded as a section of science, an excellent adventure, and as a section of art. This chapter will take us through the following:

a) How we can install Python Program on our computers and laptops

b) How people can print next to the screen

c) What comments imply to and how people can apply them

d) How we can use Python's IDLE, an integrated development environment, to write, edit, operate, and to store our Programs

Setting Up Python on Windows

The easiest way to put Python on your computer is to launch the Windows Store, search for Python on the search bar and install it. At the time of writing, the Python Software Foundation claims the

Windows Store version might have stability issues. If you have some issues with running this version or you are using an older Windows operating system version, you have to take the traditional route by going to the official Python Software Foundation website at python.org and head to the Windows download section where you can see the latest links.

Setting Up Python on Other Operating Systems

Python cannot be found in the macOS App Store so you need to obtain the installer from the official website as well. In fact the same website has various other versions of Python for other including Linux, Solaris, VMS and even iOS. Avoid older versions of Python as they may contain bugs and don't bother with any alpha or beta releases because they are reserved for testers who don't mind sacrificing stability for cutting-edge features.

Initiating the Game Over Program

Game Over portrays the two main notorious words applied in computer gaming. The console window from a computer game can only exhibit text, but although not as perfect as that one displayed by the GUI. The console uses are more facile to note and are a better position for the starting programmer to begin.

The Game Over project is passably uncomplicated: it is one of the most manageable Python Program a person can consider writing about. After completing this advanced Python project, you will have to encompass all the planned activities needed to start a Python Programming, and this may involve installing Python language on your computer system. You will also toil through all the procedures of writing, storing, and operating a Python program. The moment all these are completed, then we would be ready to run comprehensive programs with more details.

Introducing the Python IDLE

Python is obtained with a GUI-coalesce growth environment known as the IDLE. A development environment is inferred as a set of objects that enables writing programs to be more straightforward. A person may ponder of it as a word processor for his/her programs. But it implies to more than a position that a person notes, store, and edit his/her work. IDLE offers two modes in which a person can work from: this could provide a communication mode and a text mode.

Programming in Interactive Mode

Eventually, we can say that it is now time to access some Python programming information in details. The fastest means is to commence with Python in communicative mode. With this mode, a person may instruct Python what he/she wants it to perform, and automatically, Python will deliver it immediately.

Writing Your First Program

To start with your commutative session, beginning from the menu, opt for Programs, Python 2.2, IDLE. The window that is referred to us the Python Shell can appear a bit dissimilar from that illustrated in the screenshot of a person's computer. At the order prompt depicted as (>>>), you need to type: and then print the word "Game Over." The decipherer replies by exhibiting on the screen. *Tada!* With this, it could imply that you have already noted your first Python program! Here you would be the real programmer with a bit more information to learn, but that would apply to all people.

Using the print Statement

To use the print statement effectively, you will have to take more time looking at the line you entered, print "Game Over." Then keenly try to take account on how direct it is to apply. With no prior information on programming, you may have presumably estimated what it performs. That would mean Python in brief; it is incisive and clear so that people can easily understand it. You will come to cherish more of these when you can to learn how Python is complicated a little bit in the coming chapters and topics. This print assertion exhibits whatever message a person can type between the set of the quotes. A person can also apply it by itself to print a free line.

Learning the Jargon

Now that you have known some information, you have become a programmer, and you will have to use some of the technical words that programmers use and understand. The line that you have just keyed in the decipherer has referred to us the statement or the assertion. In the English language, the term statement applies to a full thought. On the other hand, in Python, the word statement refers to a complete specification. This is to imply that it performs a specific task. So, the print word "Game Over"   I suggest to a statement.

The assertion that you have just inserted is created by two sections. The first one is referred to as the command. It functions only as the verb does since it illustrates/tells the PC what action it should perform or take. In our case, it seems to say to the computer to exhibit text on the screen of your computer. Python is case-sentient of to orders and is in lowercase. For this, it is quite clear that print "Game Over" will function quite well, while Print "Game Over" and PRINT "Game Over" won't even work in the first place. The second section of the assertion, "Game Over," implies an expression. It does not perform something, but it is something. A perfect mean to ponder over this would regard it as an expression that contains a value. The value like that one listed in the phrase "Game Over," or even the values in the number 17 would be a perfect example for one to think of when interpreting statements. An expression may also measure some values like 2 + 5, which is an expression that ascribes to the digit to 7.

In this situation, a person may be even more peculiar by stating that "Game Over" implies a string expression. This would mean that it is a series of features, like the ones that are on the keyboard. The string can be like an odd identify text or words which may be more precise, but at the same time, the identity is derived from the concept of the text in a string or a series of features. Not only do people acknowledge about jargon, but also do they you have some trivia under their belt now too. Now that you have become a perfect programmer, you may apprise someone that you noted some Python code. Codes imply the programming assertions. A person may apply to function just like the verb; through this, a person can state that they were up all night eating Doritos, drinking Jolt Cola, and coding like a lunatic.

Generating an Error

Computers draw everything as they come without applying any logic. So if a person misspells an order by even just a single letter, the PC will have completely no idea of what that person's mean. For instance, at the communicative prompt, I typed print "Game Over." The interpret replied with a Syntax Error: invalid syntax. Transcribed to the English language, the decipherer is saying "Huh?!" It does not understand the print. As a human being, a person may assume my typo and acknowledge what I intended to say. The PCs are not so forgiving, this mistake in my assertion, called a *bug* in a program, acquires me an error text and no single thing else printed on the computer screen. Typically this is referred to as a syntax error, implying that the PC does not acknowledge anything. Syntax mistakes are always brought about by a typo and are in most occasions simple to fix.

Understanding Color Coding

A person can observe that words that appear on the computer screen are printed in various colors. The colors coding assist a person to swiftly understand what he/she has typed by visually grouping them accordingly. And there is a methodology for this coloring madness. Single words, such as the same print, are illustrated in orange color. Strings, like "Game Over," are displayed in green color. As people write extensive projects, this color program will come in handy. It will assist them in obtaining their code in a single glance.

Programming in Script Mode

Applying the communicative mode allows a person to obtain an immediate response. This would be better since that person may perceive the outcome of the assertion in the same time. But it is not structured to develop programs that people can store and operate later. Python's IDLE also proffers a text mode, in which we can note, edit, load, and save our programs. It is more similar to a word processor for a person's code. We can do familiar tasks as find and replace, and cut and paste more easily here.

- *Writing Your First Program*

A person may open a text-mode window from the interactive window he/she have using. Select the document menu, preceded by the New Window, after doing this a new window will pop up. Now you can write print "Game Over" and click Enter. What happens? Nothing! This is because you may be in the script mode. What only you are performing here is typing a list of assertions for the PC to implement later. The moment you save your project, you can operate it.

- *Saving and Running Your Program*

To store/save a person's program, select File, then Save As. Then proceed to give your File a name, and you can even give it the name game_over.2019.py. You can also make it easier by saving it to your desktop. To operate your Game Over program, you quickly need to select Edit, Run Script, the script here may be just the name of another program. Then proceed with, the interactive window since your active window displays the outcomes of your program.

First, you will observe that the communicative window has the old message from before. That it still contains the assertion you inserted while in the interactive mode, print "Game Over," and the results, the text Game Over. However, a person needs to trap and operate his/her program from IDLE like it was done before to save the program. If in case you do not do this, IDLE will show you a Not Saved dialog box.

The trick in the interactive mode is perfect for attempting a small concept quickly. Script mode is excellent for noting programs a person can run later. Applying both patterns together is an excellent means to code. Even though a person may require only script mode to note a project, we usually store an interactive window open while we code. Besides, we write programs in script mode, skip over to the interactive window to attempt a concept that can work or be assured the application of command is performed in the right manner. In most occasions, the text window is the place people craft their final project. The interactive window becomes a scratchpad where they can ponder about other things and experiment them there. Applying them together aids people to note good projects more efficiently.

Using Comments

The proceedings are the first three lines of the program:

Game Over

Demonstrates the print command

Michael Dawson - 12/26/02

Explanations

These lines are not assertion for the PC to implement as people may think. The fact of the matter here is that even the computer typically assumes them. These notes are referred to like the comments and are mostly meant for us. They explain programming code in the English language or any other language. Comments are absent to other programmers and aid them to interpret their code. Also, they assist a person to recall how they completed something that was not comprehensible at first glance.

A person also develops a comment with the digit symbol, #. Anything after this sign except those in a string is comments. Comments are assumed by the PC. You also need to know that comments are always colored red in IDLE to make them stand out. It is a perfect concept to begin all of your projects with a bit of comment since it becomes essential in listing the titles of the program; the programmer is supposed to write and date them accurately.

People could be thinking: "Why have comments at all? Since we wrote the program, so we acknowledge what it performs." That could be correct months later after they type their codes, but professional programmers know that after a few months away from a project, their original intents could not be as explicit. If you need maybe to redefine an old program, a few well- placed comments could make your work easier.

Using Blank Lines

Technically, the proceeding line in the program is blank. The PC, in most cases, assumes the blank lines; these, are just meant are meant to aid human reading of codes. Blank lines may result in a more accessible interpretation of programs. In most occasions, they are stored as associated with codes and as isolated parts with a blank line. In this program, I isolated the comments from the print assertions with a blank line.

Printing the String

The following line should appear familiar to you since it has been discussed over and over in the first Chapter:

```
print "Game Over."
```

It is your old pal, the print expression. This line, just as it runs the communicative mode, prints Game Over.

Waiting for the User

The final line of the program (raw_input("\n\nPress the enter key to exit."), typically exhibits the prompt, click the enter button to exit, and wait for the user to activate the Enter key. The moment the user clicks on the button, the program terminates. This is a perfect trick to store a console window open until the user is finished with an application.

Chapter Two

Categories, Variables, and Simple I/O: The Useless Trivia Program

Now that we have acknowledged the primary storing and implementing programs, it's the time to learn deeper and develop more understanding of Python Programs. In this section, come across varies means PCs could group and keep the information, and more fundamentally, how to apply this information in your Project. A person will perceive how to access data from the user; this will enable him/her programs become communicative, primarily when he/she studies the proceeding activities

- Apply triple-quoted strings and escape pattern to get more manage over the message
- Create your projects do math
- Store information in the PC's memory
- Apply variables to acquire and manipulate that information
- Access input from users to develop communicative programs

Initiating the Game Over 2.0 Program

Game Over 2.0 enhances upon its predecessor program, Game Over, by exhibiting a more spectacular form of the similar text that illustrates a player that his or her PC game has reached its end. Applying one and double quotes cause the outcome to be always more visually appealing.

The code for the program tells that it is quite easy to present message applying the quotes in various means:

```
# Game Over - Version 2
# Illustrates the utility of quotes in strings # Michael Dawson - 1/9/03
print "Program 'Game Over' 2.0" print \
"""

"""

raw_input("\n\nClick the enter key to exit.")
```

Using Quotes Inside Strings

After learning how to develop simple strings by neighboring message with quotes, we can now apply either a set of a single (' ') or double quotes (" ") to develop string values. Note that the PC does not care. This implies that 'Game Over' is exactly similar to the string also presented as "Game Over." Meanwhile, a person can have a look at the initial mien of a string in the program:

```
print "Program 'Game Over' 2.0."
```

This assertion seems to apply both sorts of quotes. It is only the one quote that shows up, since they are section of the string, just like the letter G., on the other hand, the double quotes are not a section of the string, since they are like bookends, illustrating to the PC where the string starts and terminates. So, if people are applying a set of double quotes to "bookend" their string, then they can apply as many single quotes inside the string as they would like. Besides, if they neighbor their strings with a set of single quotes, they can apply as many double quotes inside the string as they would wish to apply.

The moment a person has applied a single sort of quote as bookends for his/her string, that person cannot use that form of the quote inside his or her line. This makes some sense, since the moment the PC discerns the second appearance of the quote that started the string, it ponders the string is over. For instance, "With the statement, 'Houston, we have an issue.' Tom Lovell since one of our most popular astronauts." is a correct string. But, with the assertions, "Houston, we have an issue." Tom Lovell since one of our most popular astronauts." Is not correct, since the moment the PC perceives the second double quote, it ponders that the string is complete. So, the PC discerns that the string "With the statement," proceeded by the statement, Houston. And since the PC has no thought what Houston is, a person will obtain a nasty syntax error.

Using Quotes with Strings

Assumingly I think that you were able to see the sample of a string, "Game Over," in the previous chapter one. Strings may become much extended and more complicated. A person may need to accord a user many paragraphs of specification, or even need to format his or her message/information in a very particular meaning that is preferred by him or her. Applying quotes may assist people in developing various strings to perpetuate all of this information.

Continuing a Statement on the Next Line

The following line of code, print \, appears lonely. And it actually should look that way, since it is a full assertion. Inclusively, a person notes a single word on each line. But he or she does not have to, since that person may stretch an individual assertion across various lines. All that a person has to perform is to apply the line-continuation nature, \ which is just a backslash. Then you need to place it anywhere, in most instances, you need to apply a space, but not inside a string, to proceed with your assertion on the following line. The PC will behave as if it takes a single extended line of code. Here the main hint is that your computer does not consider how long a programming line is, but people do believe this. If for instance, your line appears to be too long, or clearer as several lines, then you would need to apply the line-continuation nature to split it up.

Creating Triple-Quoted Strings

Particularly the most cooling section of the program is where it prints out "Game Over" in a large block of message. The next string is responsible for:

" " " Game Over" " "

This is what is called a triple-quoted string. It is a string surrounded by a set of triple quotes that follows each other one after the other. As illustrated previously, it does not matter which type of quotes a person applies, provided that he/she bookend with a similar form. As a person may perceive it, a triple-quoted string may span various lines. They print on the screen of the computer exactly the way that he or she wrote them. If that person wants to print more than some lines of the message, triple-quoted strings are the preferred passage to go through.

Applying Escape Sequences with Strings

Escape patterns/sequences permit a person to place a unique feature into his or her strings. These provide a perfect way to manage the flexibility over the message is displayed on the screen of the computer. The escape pattern a person will work with to create the two characters: a backslash proceeded by another nature. This can allow all look a bit peculiar, but the moment that person perceives some patterns action; he/she will notice how simple they are to apply.

Initiating the Fancy Credits Program

Besides apprising a player that the game is over, a project occasionally displays credits, a chart of all the individuals who toiled so hard to achieve their desires. Fancy Credits applies escape patterns to attain some effects and always cannot function without them. The code may appear a little cryptic when you first look at them, below are the examples of how they appear:

> *# Fancy Credits*
> *# illustrates escape pattern # Michael Dawson 1/11/03*
> *# sound the model bell print "\a"*
> *print "\t\t\tFancy Credits"*
> *print "\t\t\t \\ \\ \\ \\ \\ \\ \\" print "\t\t\t\tby"*
> *print "\t\t\tMichael Dawson"*
> *print "\t\t\t \\ \\ \\ \\ \\ \\ \\" print "\nSpecial thanks is directed out to:"*
> *print "My hairstylist, Tom \'The Better\', who never says \"can\'t\"."*
> *raw_input("\n\nClick the enter key to exit.")*
> *don't worry you will actually understand these very soon.*

Sounding the System Bell

Upon operating this plan, a person will realize something dissimilar immediately. The very initial assertion in the program always creates noise. The print "\a" sounds the model bell of a person's PC. It performs via the escape pattern, \a, which illustrates the model bell nature. Each moment a person print it, the bell then proceeds by ringing. A person may also print a string with just this pattern, as I have, or he or she can place it inside an extended string. That person

20

may even apply the design various times to ring the bell more than one moment.

Moving Forward a Tab Stop

Often people will need to put some message off from the left edge where it always prints. In a statement processor, people can apply the Tab button. With strings, a person may apply the escape pattern for a tab, \t. That's exactly what has been done in the next line:

print "\t\t\tFancy Credits"

We applied tab escape pattern, \t, three times in a row. So, the moment the project prints the string, it prints three tabs ago and then followed by the Fancy Credits. This result to the Fancy Credits, to look closely centered in the console window. Tab patterns are better for pairing off message, as in this program, but they are also better for organizing the information into columns.

Printing a Backslash

If perhaps you have pondered ahead, wondering how to print a backslash if the PC usually elucidates a backslash as the starting of an escape pattern. Well, the solution for this issue is quite easy: you need to apply the two backslashes in a row. Each of the preceding two lines prints three tabs, as a product of the three \t sequences:

print "\t\t\t \\ \\ \\ \\ \\ \\ \\ \\" print "\t\t\t \\ \\ \\ \\ \\ \\ \\ \\"

Then, every print has exactly eight backslashes, which are isolated by spaces. Do you want to confirm then go ahead you will find eight sets of backslashes, which are then isolated by spaces?

Inserting a Newline

The newline pattern is an essential sequence at a person's disposal, which is always represented by \n. By applying this pattern, a person may insert a newline nature into his or her strings for a blank line where he/she wants it. Newlines are commonly applied straight at the beginning of a string to isolate it from the message last printed. That is what is shown in the next line:

print "\nSpecial thanks directed out to:"

The PC discerns the \n sequence, prints a blank line, then prints Special thanks directed out to This assertion is equal to the preceding two expressions:

print
print "Special thanks directed out to:"

Inserting a Quote

Entering a quote into a string, not forgetting its form you applied to bookend it, is incomprehensible. imply "set a quote in this place," and would not probably make an error, with the PC as an indicator for the close of your line. This is what was applied to obtain both types of quotes on one edge of the message:

print "My hairstylist, Tom \'The Better\', who never says \"can\'t\.""

The set of double quotes at both terminals are the bookends, describing the string. To create the string simpler to interpret, search at it in this section:

- \'The Better\' prints as 'The Better'

- Every \' sequence is printed as a one quote

- \"can\'t\" prints as "can't"

- Both \" sequences print as dual quotes The lone \' sequence prints as a one quote

As a person may perceive, escape pattern are not so bad the moment you have perceived them in action. And they may come in quite handy means.

The following illustrates some examples of selected escape sequences and their description:

Sequence   **Description**
- **a)** \\   Backslash. Prints a single backslash.
- **b)** \'   one quote. Print one quote.
- **c)** \"   Dual quote. Prints a double quote.
- **d)** \a   Bell. Sounds the system bell.
- **e)** \b   Backspace. Moves the cursor back with a single space.
- **f)** \n   Newline. Moves cursor to start next line.
- **g)** \t   Horizontal tab. Moves cursor forward one tab stop

Initiating the Silly Strings Project/Program

The Silly Strings projects prints multiple of strings on the screen of the computer. Though people have already perceived the strings printed, how these strings were developed is brand-new to people. Have a look at the following code:

```
# Silly Strings
# illustrates string concatenation and repetition
```

```
# Michael Dawson - 1/11/03
print "A person may concatenate two " + "strings with the '+' processor."
print "\nThis string " + "may not " + "seem terr" + "simply impressive. "
\
+ "But what " + "a person don't know," + " is that " + "it's one real" \
+ "l" + "y" + " long string, developed from the concatenation " \
+ "of " + "thirty-two " + "different strings, broken across " \
+ "nine lines." + " Now are a person" + " impressed?\n\n" + "See, " \
+ "even newlines may be implanted into a single string, making" \
+ " it appear " + "as " + "if " + "it" + "'s " + "got " + "to " \
+ "be" + " many strings." + " Okay, now this " + "one " \
+ "long" + " string " + "is over!"
print \
""""
```

If a person the same as a string, he/she may replicate it. For instance, who does not like pie? That's correct, none of you. But if anyone of you likes it, then he/she should say it like they mean it:""",

```
print "Pie" * 10
print "\nNow that's good eating." raw_input("\n\nClick the enter key to exit.")
print "\nNow that's good eating." raw_input("\n\nPress the enter key to exit.")
```

Concatenating Strings

Concatenating strings refers to connecting strings together to develop an entire brand-new string. An easy example is illustrated in the first print assertion below:

```
print "A person may concatenate two " + "strings with the '+' processor."
```

The + processor links the two strings, " A person may concatenate two " and "strings with the '+' processor.", in conjunction to make a brand-new, an extended string. It is exceedingly intuitive since it's like attaching the strings in conjunction applying a similar sign that is always used for appending numbers. The main trap here would be the moment a person connects two strings, where their real values are blended together, with no gap or separator nature entered between them. So, if we were to link the two strings "cup" and "cake", we would close up with "cupcake" and not "cup cake". In most instances, people would need to enter a space between strings that people connect, so that they do not forget to insert them in. The following print assertion illustrates that a person can concatenate 'till your heart's content:

```
print "\nThis string " + "can not " + "seem terr" + "ibly impressive. " \
+ "But what " + "a person does not know," + " is that " + "it's one real" \
+ "l" + "y" + " extended string, developed from the concatenation " \
+ "of " + "thirty-two " + "various strings, broken across " \
+ "nine lines." + " Now are you" + " impressed?\n\n" + "See, " \
+ "even newlines may be implanted into one string, making" \
+ " it appear " + "as " + "if " + "it" + "'s " + "got " + "to " \
+ "be" + " various strings." + " Okay, now this " + "one " \
+ "long" + " string " + "is over!"
```

The PC prints a single extended string that was developed first by the concatenation of 32 individual strings. One particular issue that a person can realize here is that the string does not accurately wrap in the console window of the computer. So you need to take precaution every time you develop super-long strings on your computer as this can give a lot of issues you don't know how to deal with them.

Suppressing a Newline

We have learned how we may append additional newlines with the \n escape pattern. Besides this, we can also suppress a newline so that the message of two continuous print assertions pops up on the same line. All that a person has to do is to append a comma at the terminal of a print assertion, like so:

print \ """"

If strings are good, then we can continue performing them repeatedly. For an instant, who does not like pie? That's correct, none of you. By adding the comma at the end of this triple-quoted string, the next text printed will appear on the same line as say it as you mean it:

Repeating Strings

The proceeding new concept presented in the program is shown in the next line:

*print "Pie" * 10*

This line develops a brand-new string, "Pie Pie Pie Pie Pie Pie Pie Pie Pie Pie," and prints it out. That's the string "Pie" replicated10 times. Like the concatenation processor, the replication processor, *, is excellent intuitive. It is the similar sign applied for multiplying digits on a PC, so a person needs to repeat a string with it creates sense.

Working with Numbers

Computers allow people to represent data in other means. One of the most core means that networks represent information through the use of numbers, which are applied for almost all program. Whether typing a gap/space shooter game or home finance package, people need to illustrate numbers in one way or another. They need to get high scores or even halt their account balances. Fortunately, Python contains various categories of numbers which can be suitable for all games or utilization of programming wants.

Initiating the Statement Problems Program

The word problem program applies the dreaded assertions problems, which always seems to incorporate two trains departing separate cities at a similar time but going at opposite directions. You need not be frightened, as you will actually solve this problem or even calculate any math's here since the computer will all that for you. All that a person required to do is to press the enter button and let the PC do the rest.

The sources of code for the program include:

 # Word Problems
 # Illustrates numbers and math # Michael Dawson 1/12/03
print \ """

If an expecting hippo, weighing 3,000 pounds, gives birth to a 100-pound calf, but then eats 50 pounds of food, how much does she weigh?""" raw_input("Press the enter key to find out.")

print "3000 - 100 + 50 = ",
print 3000 - 100 + 50
print \ """

If a scholar returns from successful research and buys every of 6 companions three bottles of soda, how many bottles does the scholar purchase?

*""" raw_inputprint "6 * 3 = ",*

*print 6 * 3*

print \ """

If a child has 24 slices of oranges and eats six slices a day, how many days will the orange last?"""

raw_input("Click the enter button to find out.") print "24 / 6 = ",

print 24 / 6

print \ """

If a team of 4 pilots finds a chest full of 107 gold coins, and they split the booty evenly, how many coins will be left over?

""" raw_input("Click the enter button to find out.")

print "107 % 4 = ",

print 107 % 4

print \ """

If a restaurant halt comes to 19 dollars with tip, and you and your pal divided it evenly four ways, how much do you each throw in?

""" raw_input("Press the enter key to find out.")

print "19 / 4 = ",

print 19 / 4 print "WRONG!"

raw_input("Click the enter button for the right answer.") print 19.0 / 4

raw_input("\n\nClick the enter key/button to exit.")

Using Mathematical Operators

With a mathematical processor, a person may turn his or her PC into a costly calculator. The processors should appear a bit familiar. For instance, the proceeding line

print 2000 - 100 + 50

What you need to do is to subtract 100 from 2000 and then follow adding 50 before printing the answer of 1950. Technically, it calculates the assertion 2000 − 100 + 50, which is equivalent to 1950. An expression is referred to as a pattern of values, connected by the processor, which may be untangled to another value.

> *The line*
>   *print 6 * 3*
>   *multiplies six by 3 and prints the answer of 18.*
> *The line*
>   *print 24 / 6*
>   *Divides 24 by 6 and prints the answer of 4.*
>   *Pretty normal stuff. But halt out the following calculation:*
>   *print 107 % 4*

Utilizing % as a mathematical processor is presumably new to a person. Applied here, the sign % present modulus, which is just a fancy mean of stating, "get me the leftover number." So 107 % 4 calculates to the leftover digit of 107 / 4, which is 3. But if every individual sets 4 dollars in, that's the sum of only 16, not 19. And that evacuates the waitperson short three bucks. What will happen? Well, the moment Python runs integer division, the outcome is usually an integer. So, any fractional segment is assumed. If a person needs floating-point division, or what some individuals refer certain division, where at least one of the numbers must be a floating-point number. The proceeding lines outcomes inaccurate division:

> *print 19.0 / 4*

Understanding Numeric Types

The program Word Problems utilizes numbers on most occasions, and this is always palpable, the only thing that may not be clear is that it applies two distinct forms of digits. Python permit programmers to apply various models of numbers. Python programmers apply two main forms of numbers in their program, where the most common forms used are integers and floating-point numbers. Integers are referred to as whole numbers without any part of fractional in them. You can also refer to integers as numbers without a decimal. Integer numbers include 1, 3, 76, -987m among others, provided that a number has no decimal. Floats-points are numbers with a decimal point they are exactly the opposite of integer; they include 3.976, -809.1, and 1.0.

The following examples summarize the mathematical operators with integers

Operator	Description	Example	Answer
• *	Multiplication	7 * 2	14
• /	Division	7 * 2	3
• +	Addition	7 + 2	9
• -	Subtraction	7 - 2	5

The following are summarize the mathematical processor with floating-point numbers

Operator	Description	Example	Answer
• *	Multiplication	7.0 * 2.0	14.0
• /	Division	7.0 * 2.0	3.0
• +	Addition	7.0 + 2.0	9.0
• -	Subtraction	7.0 - 2.0	5.0

Understanding Variables

Via variables, a person can keep and handle text, a primary concept of programming. Python allows people to develop variables to arrange and access this data.

Initiating the Greeter Program

From just a screenshot of the computers, the program to appears like something a person could have already noted. But within the code skulk the entire, new, robust idea of variables. Have a look here:

> *Greeter*
> *# illustrates the application of a variable # Michael Dawson 1/13/03*
> *name = "Nelson" print name*
> *print "Hi, " + name*
> *raw_input("\n\nClick the enter button to exit.")*

Creating Variables

A variable proffers a mean to mark and access the text. Rather than of getting to acknowledge exactly the place in the PC's memory, some data is kept, a person applies a variable to arrive at it. It is your pal on his cell phone. You click a key, and you would get to your friend. But before you apply a variable, you must develop it, as in the proceeding line:

> *name = "Larry"*

This line is referred to as an assignment assertion. It develops a variable called name and allots it the value "Larry." To sum it up, assignment assertion give a value to a variable. If the variable does not exist, like in the case of name, it's created, and then assigned the value.

Using Variables

The moment a variable has been developed, it refers to some value. The comfort and strength of variables are that they may be applied just like the values of the variables. So the line print name

Prints the string "Nelson" just like the assertion print "Nelson" performs. And the line

print "Hi, " + name

Concatenates the values "Hellow," and "Nelson" to develop a new string, "Hellow, Nelson.", and prints it out. The products are similar to the outcome of print "Hi," + "Larry."

Naming Variables

Acting like a grateful guardian of your project, you may select the identity of your variables at any time. You can also select name from any category like names of people, alphabet, or even numbers. With these names, the programs will quickly run, however, the only thing you have to do is to adhere to specific variable rules to develop and run a legal variable name. If for instance, you go and design an illegal one, Python will automatically show you this and even illustrate the error you have made while developing the illegal variable names. The following is some of the rules that one should adhere to while creating a variable identity:

a) The first rule state that a mutable character or name must only have letters, numbers, and underscores; nothing else should be added to them.

b) The second rule state that a variable name or identity cannot begin with a number; instead it suggests that it can start with letters or underscores.

Besides the regulations of developing legal variable identities or names, the following are a few guidelines that professional programmers use when developing a perfect variable identity to make their work easy. The reason why programmers apply these rules is that once they have programmed the rules for a while, they know the Gulf of dissimilarity that exists between useful variables and legal variables. Any person naming any variable name must follow the guidelines illustrated below. However, you should never begin with a variable alpha7345690876. The guidelines include:

- Opt for descriptive names or identity when naming variable. You should ensure that variable identities or names should be perspicuous enough to enable another programmer to glance at the name and form a perfect concept of what it may represent. For instance, a person needs to use a score rather than s. Perhaps one exception that this particular rule incorporates variables applied for a short or brief period. Generally, programs provide those variables with short names, such as x. That's okay since by using x, the program comprehensively sends the variable to stand for a quick holding place.

- You should be consistent in the process of naming your variables since there are a variety of ideologies of how a person can note multiword variable names in their programs when using Python. For instance, which one would you consider being correct among the two, Is it high score or high_score?

The style applied here is the underscore style. But this is not important since the method a method used is not considered as search; what matters is the consistency of a person.

- Another important guideline that a person should consider in the naming of variable m is that he/she should follow the traditions of the language of Python; this is so because some naming protocols are just traditional. For instance, in many languages, including Python, variable names, or identities begins with a small letter. Another tradition is to circumvent applying an underscore as the fundamental nature of your variable identity since names that start with an underscore have unique implication in Python.

- Finally, you need to keep the length of your variable in scrutiny. Although, this may appear to be going against your initial guideline set in the first point, "Choose descriptive names." For instance, you may ask yourself. Is checking account balance a perfect variable name? Maybe not, because extended variable names or identities may sometimes lead us to problems. They may make expressions/statements challenging to read. Besides this, the longer the variable name may be, the higher the possibility of a typo. As a guideline states, always try to maintain your variable names or identities to be below 15 characters.

Getting User Input

After cherishing all that the Python programs or projects that have been offered here in this book, a person can still be pondering of what he or she will doing in the next step. He/she doesn't have to worry.

Since writing programs that operate the same way this book commands, always does this without experiencing any problems that come when creating fancy variables. But for a person to run fundamentally crucial things, that would incorporate getting, saving or storing, and handling user input, that person may need variables. For more information on the Greeter program, you need to check out the following topic to get more insight into the subject and gain a deeper understanding.

Initiating Personal Greeter Program

The Personal Greeter program to your PC on Python appends a single element that is very cool to the Greeter program in user input. Rather than you are working with a predefined value, that the PC always allows the user to enter his or her name or identity and then applies the identity to say Hi or Hello. This is still illustrated on the screen of the computer.

You will notice that obtaining user input is not that very hard. As a product, the code does not appear much different from each other:

 # Personal Greeter
 # Illustrates obtaining user input # Michael Dawson 1/13/03
name = raw_input("Hi. What's your name? ") print name
print "Hi, " + name
Applying the raw_input() Function
raw_input("\n\nClick the enter button to exit.")
The only line that's changed is the assignment expression or statement:
name = raw_input("Hi. What's your name? ")

The left side of the assertion is exactly similar as in the Greeter program. Name is developed, and value is allotted to it, just like

35

before. But this moment, the value is not a line that was distributed. It is the line value of whatever the user inserts. On the other hand, on the right side of the task assertion is a request to the role raw_input(). A position is similar to a mini- project that runs off and performs some specified activity. The purpose of raw_input() is to obtain a few messages from the user. Sometimes a person may provide role values to apply. He or she may set these values, known as arguments, between the brackets. In instance, the single dissension conveyed to raw_input() is the string "Hi or Hellow. What's your name? "raw_input() applies the line to evoke the user. raw_input() interludes for the user to insert something. The moment the user clicks the Enter button, raw_input() gains whatever the user writes, as a string. That's the line that the identity obtains.

If you are still not explicit on the way this functions, you can ponder of it this in this manner: applying raw_input() is similar to ordering a pizza in a restaurant. The raw_input() role is similar to a pizza parlor. You can create a request to a pizza parlor to a location that your order comes from, and a person creates a request to all the raw_input() role to boot it into gear. The moment a person requests for the pizza parlor, he or she can offer data, like "pepperoni." The moment he or she requires for the raw_input() role, you run it in the argument, "Hi. What's your name?". After you complete your request for the pizza parlor, the workers will supply a pepperoni pizza to your door. After you mat and then called to raw_input(), the role returns whatever string the user has entered on the button. The remaining Personal Greeter program functions just like the Greeter program. It creates no difference to the PC, as it is a means of having name value. Thus the string:

print name

prints the value of the character or name. While the line

print "Hi, " + name

Concatenates the "Hi," and the value of identity, and prints this brand-new line out. At this juncture, a person may acknowledge adequate to understand the final line in all of these console programs. The end line aims to hold up for the user to click the Enter button:raw_input("\n\nClick the enter button to exit.")

It operates precisely in that way via the raw_input() role. Because we don't account for what the user enters in his computers, provided that he or she clicks the Enter button, we don't allocate the get back value of raw_input() to a variable like that was determined before. It can look eerie to obtain a value and perform nothing with it, but that will depend on a person's option. If a person doesn't allocate the get back value to a variable, the PC assumes it. So, the moment the user clicks the Enter button, the program classes, and the console window end.

Using String Methods

Indeed Python contains a copious set of pieces of equipment for toiling with lines or strings. One particular model of these pieces of equipment is string methodology. String models or type let an individual develop a new series from the previous string. A person may perform all the possible thing from the simple and these things may include creating a string that contains only capital-letters the form of the original string, and to the complicated one; such as developing a brand-new string that is as an outcome a series of tangle letter replacements.

Initiating the Quotation Manipulation Program

"The art of prognostication is very hard, specifically with the honor of the future." This statement is, according to Mark Twain. Indeed no person can precisely prophesy about the future, but it is still amazing to read the forecast that sages have developed about technology. An excellent example to illustrate in this place would be, "I thought there was a global market for about five PCs," which was altered by then IBM chairman, Thomas Watson, back in 1943. The quotation operating the programs that were used to write the prints in this quote was acquired using several string methods. Fortunately, we have been able to note this program since we happen to have computer #3.

Below is the code for the program:

```
# Quotation Manipulation
# Illustrating methods # Michael Dawson 1/11/03
# quote from IBM Chairman, Thomas Watson, back in 1943
quote = "I thought there is a global market for about five PCs." print
"Original quote:"
print quote
print "\nIn capital letters:" print quote.upper()
print "\nIn small letters:" print quote.lower()
print "\nAs a title:" print quote.title()
print "\nWith a small substitution:"
print quote.substitute("five", "millions of")
print "\nOriginal quote is still:" print quote
raw_input("\n\nClick the enter button to exit.")
```

Developing New Strings with String Methods

There is a brand-new ideology at work; the code in the strings can still greatly be understandable. Look at the next the line: *print quote.upper()*

A person may approximate what the code performs: print a form of the quote in all capital letters. The line runs this via the application of a string system illustrated as, *upper()*. A string system or method is like the capability a string has. This would mean that a quote can develop a new string, a capitalized form of itself, via its upper() strategy. The moment it runs this, it gets back to this new string, and the line will look like the following line:

> *print "I THOUGHT THERE IS A GLOBAL MARKET FOR ABOUT FIVE COMPUTERS."*

The string of the code does not always appear like this, but any individual may ponder of it in this manner to assist him or her in understanding how the strategy or method functions. An individual may probably realize what the parentheses in this method require; this should remind this person the roles that we have just studied in this chapter. Methods are the same as function, and the only difference is that a built-in role or function, such as raw_input(), may be referred to on its own. While a string method or strategy must be called via a specific string. It would make sense to write the following line:

> *print upper()*

Here you have kicked off a method or let's say a strategy, by attaching a dot, the proceeded by the identity of the strategy or method, then again proceeded by a set of brackets, after a string value. The brackets are not meant just for. Just as the functions, a person can send arguments inside them. upper(). This does not acquire any arguments but takes with the replace() as we shall see this in the example below.

The line
print quote.lower()

Invokes the lower() strategy of the quote to develop all-lowercase-letters forms, which it obtains back to. Then, that brand-new, lowercase string is printed.

The line
print quote.title()

Always prints the form of a quote that looks like a title. The title() strategy gets back to a place the first letter of every statement is written in capital letters, while the remaining string is in lowercase.

The line
print quote.replace("five", "millions of")
prints a brand-new string, where each occurrence of "five" in a quote is substituted with "millions of."

The strategy of replacing () requires at least two sections of data, that is the old information to be substituted, and the new information that substitutes it. Any person using this method must be able to differentiate the two arguments using a comma. That person can also add an optional third argument that is *an integer*, which tells the method the highest number of times it can apply to make a substitution. Finally, the program will print a quote once more containing: *print "\nOriginal quote is still:" print quote*

The following example illustrates quotes that do not change. You need to take notice that a string method makes a new string, which does not affect the original string.

The method or the strategy	Descriptions
Title ()	Gets back to a new string where the first letter of every word is capitalized, and all the rest are lowercase.
[, max])	Gets back to a new string where occurrences of the string old are substituted with the string new. The optional max curbs the number of substitution.
upper()	Gets back to the uppercase form of the string
swapcase()	Gets back to a new string where the case of every letter is switched. Uppercase becomes lowercase, and lowercase becomes uppercase
Lower ()	Gets back to the lowercase form of the string.
Capitalize ()	Gets back to a new string where the initial letter is capitalized, and the remaining once are lowercase.
Strip ()	Gets back to a string where all the white space (tabs, spaces, and newlines) at the start and end is deleted.

Using the Right Types

Up to this juncture, we have applied three various categories, including strings, integers, and floating-point numbers. It is now essential to acknowledge not only the kind of information that is present to us but also the way to work with them properly.

Initiating the Trust Fund Buddy-Bad Program

The concept of this program was developed to create an appliance for those souls that play all day long, living off a kind trust fund. The program is made to enumerate a grand sum for monthly usage based on each user input. This grand sum is made available to assist those individuals who are living beyond any reasonable ways and lives to stay within expenditure so as they do not ever have to ponder about having a real job. The Trust Fund Buddy-Bad does not function as the program had planned.

Furthermore, the program is not bluntly functioning in the right manner, since it has a bug. But it also obvious that it is not a bug that is responsible for it to collide, like in the syntax mistake experienced in chapter one of this book. The moment a program results in unintended products, but it does not collide, it then concluded that it cloud probably have a logical error or mistake. Based on what we already know that a person may be in a position to figure out what is taking place by looking at the code. Below is the list for this:

```
# Trust Fund Buddy – Bad
# Illustrates a logical mistake or error # Michael Dawson - 1/14/03
print \ """
Trust Fund Buddy
```

The sum of a person's monthly expenditure to that of his or her trust fund does not run out (then that person is forced to get a real job).

Please enter the called, monthly expenditure that you may need for a particular month. Since you are wealthy, you will have to assume the pennies amount of cash but instead opt to use only dollar amounts, since using dollars is the category that you fit in properly.

```
"""
staff = raw_input("Staff (butlers, doctor,teacher, assistant): ")
master = raw_input("Personal Master and Coach: ")
games = raw_input("PC Games: ")
total = car + rent + jet + presents + food + staff + master + games print
"\nGrand        Total: " + total
raw_input("\n\nClick the enter key to exit.")
car = raw_input("Lamborghini Tune-Ups: ")
rent = raw_input("Manhattan flat: ") jet = raw_input("Particular Jet
Rental: ") gifts = raw_input("Gifts: ")
food = raw_input("Dining Out: ")
```

Tracking Down Logical Errors or Mistakes

In most occasions it is argued that logical errors or mistakes may be one of the hardest bugs to be corrected. Unlike syntax errors and runtime errors you won't know that something is wrong at first glance because the output does not spit out an error message. Without this clue, you have to keenly observe and examine the behavior of the program and scrutinize their code appropriately. In this instance, the program's outcome illustrates the story. The vast number is explicit, not the total of all the digits the user entered. By looking at the digits, a person may perceive the sum grand printed in a concatenation of all the numbers. The main question perhaps that we should ask ourselves while dealing with this particular program would be, how did that happen? Well, if you can recall very well the raw_input() work gets back to a string. So that each number or digit that the computer user enters is treated as a string, this would mean that every variable contains a string value related to it. The role gets back a line. So every "digit number" the user enters is treated as a string. Thus, the string is not appending the number, but rather it is a concatenating the string. The line is not adding numbers.

Converting Values

The solution for this Trust Fund Buddy-Bad project is to change the line values maintained by raw_input() to numeric ones. Because the program may toil with the entire amount in dollars, it creates sense to change of every string to an integer before working with it.

Initiating the Trust Fund Buddy-Perfect Program

The Trust Fund Buddy-Good projects secure the reasonable bug in Trust Fund Buddy-Bad. Have a look here the program arrives at the accurate Total. Here is the example of how the code appears:

Trust Fund Buddy - Good
Illustrates type conversion # Michael Dawson - 1/14/03
print \
"""

Trust Fund Buddy

The sum of a person's monthly expenditure to that of his or her trust fund does not run out, and then that person is forced to get a real job.

Please enter the called, monthly expenditure that you may need for a particular month. Since you are wealthy, you will have to assume the

44

pennies amount of cash but instead opt to use only dollar amounts, since using dollars is the category that you fit in properly.

"""

car = raw_input("Lamborghini Tune-Ups: ") car = int(car)
staff = int(raw_input("Staff (butlers, doctor, chef, driver, assistant): "))
guru = int(raw_input("Personal Master or Guru and Coach: "))
games = int(raw_input("Computer Games: "))
total = car + rent + ship + gifts + food + staff + master/guru + games
print "\nGrand Total: ", total
raw_input("\n\nClick the enter button to exit.")
rent = int(raw_input("Manhattan Flats: ")) jet = int(raw_input("Private Jet Rental: ")) gifts = int(raw_input("Gifts: "))
food = int(raw_input("Dining Out: "))

Converting Strings to Integers

There are various roles that change between different categories. The role to change a value to an integer is illustrated in the following lines:
car = raw_input("Lamborghini Tune-Ups: ") car = int(car)

The initial line is just like one shown before. It gets input from the real user as a string and allots that value to car. The second line performs the conversion. The role int() takes the string referenced by car and changes it to an integer. Then, car obtains this new integer value. The following seven lines obtain and change the rests expenditure types:

rent = int(raw_input("Manhattan Apartment: ")) jet =
int(raw_input("Private Jet Rental: "))
games = int(raw_input("Computer Games: "))
gifts = int(raw_input("Gifts: "))
staff = int(raw_input("Staff (butlers, chef, techter, assistant): ")) guru =
int(raw_input("Personal Master or Guru and Coach: "))
food = int(raw_input("Dining Out: "))

Moreover, you will come to realize that the assignments are performing in just a single line now. That is since the two role calls, raw_input() and int(), are built. The nesting role request implies placing a single string inside the other. This is better as long as the get back values of the interior function may be applied by the exterior role. Here, the get back value of raw_input() is a line, and a string is a perfect a recommended category for int() to change. In the task assertion for rent, raw_input() runs out and request the user the means a person used to rent a house. The user inserts some message, and that is maintained as a string. Then, the program requests the function int() using that string. Int () gets back to the integer the string stands for. Next, the integer is allocated to rent. The other six task assertions function similarly.

Applying Augmented Task Operators

An augmented task processor is a mouthful since the idea is easy. Allow saying a person needs to acknowledge the annual amount the user uses on food. To enumerate and allocate the annual expenditure, which an individual will spend in line with: *food = food * 52*

This line proliferates the value of food by 52 and then allocates the product back to food. A person should always complete the same thing using this proceeding line: *food *= 52*

Additionally, *= is an augmented task or assignment processor, which proliferate the value of food by 52 and then allocates the outcome back to food. Giving a brand-new digit to a variable based on its initial digit is something that takes place most of the times in programming, these processors or operators offer a perfect shortcut to a general assignment.

There are other augmented tasks operators, which the fooling description summarizes, some useful ones:

Operator	Example	Equal
1. *=	x *= 5	x = x * 5
2. /=	x /= 5	x = x / 2
3. %=	x %= 5	x = x % 5
4. +=	x += 5	x = x + 5
5. -=	x -= 5	x = x – 5

Developing the Introduction Comments

Although comments do not affect, whereas the program operates, they are an essential section of each program. As usual, people list the project's reason, my name, and the date I wrote the code:

 # Useless Trivia #
 # Acquires personal data from the user and then # prints accurate, but useless facts about him or her #
 # Michael Dawson - 12/4/02

Getting the User Input

Applying for the raw_input() role, the project or program obtains the user's age, name, and weight:

name = raw_input("Hellow. What's your name? ")
age = raw_input("And how many years do you have? ") age = int(age)
weight = raw_input("Okay, last question. How various pounds do you weigh? ") weight = int(weight)

Recall, raw_input() always get back a string. Because age and weight will be treated as digits, they must be changed. I broke up this operates into two lines for every variable. First, we allocated the string from raw_input() to a variable. Then, it was changed to that string to an integer and allocated it to the variable once more.

Printing Lowercase and Uppercase Versions of the name

The next lines print a category of a name in uppercase and a form in lowercase with the aid of string strategies:

> print "\nIf poet ee cummings were to email you, and he'd address you as," name.lower()
> ee_mad = name.upper()
> print "But if ee were mad, he'd call you," ee_mad

In the uppercase category, it allocated the value to the variable ee_mad before printing them. As a person may perceive from the lowercase categories it, it's not needed to apply a variable. But we ponder it makes it explicit. Ee Cummings, by the mean, was an American poet who did not apply uppercase letters. So, if he or she was alive and emailing you, he'd correctly use all lowercase letters in a person name or identity. But if he were mad, he'd perfectly created an exception and "shout" via email by inscribing a person in uppercase.

- *Calculating dog_years*

> The user's age in dog years is enumerated and printed out:
> dog_years = age / 7
> print _\nDid you acknowledge that you're just", dog_years, "in dog years?"
> The following line joins two strings and dog_years into an extended string and exhibits it.

Enumerate seconds

The user's age, in seconds, enumerates and printed in the two next lines:

seconds = age * 365 * 24 * 60 * 60
print "But you're also over," seconds, "seconds old."

Explanation

Because there 60 seconds in a minute, 60 minutes in an hour, 24 hours in a day, and are 365 days in a year, age is proliferated by the result of 60 * 60 * 24 * 365. This value is allocated to seconds. The following line joins two strings and seconds into an extended string and exhibits it.

- *Printing name Five Times*

The program exhibits the user's name or identity five times in a row applying string replication:

called = name * 5
print "\nIf a small kid were attempting to obtain your attention, " \ "your name would become:"
print called

The variable referred is allocated the value of name, replication five times. Then, a text is printed proceeded by called.

Enumerating moon_weight and sun_weight

The following four lines enumerate and exhibit the user's weight on the moon and sun:

moon_weight = weight / 6.0

print "\nDid you acknowledge that on the moon you would weigh only,"
moon_weight, "pounds?"
sun_weight = weight * 27.1
print "But on the sun, you'd weigh," sun_weight, "(but, ah... not for long)."

Explanation

Because the gravitational force on the sun is about 27.1 times powerful than it is here on earth, I multiply the weight by and allocate the outcome to sun_weight. Again, because 27.1 is a floating-point digit, sun_weight will be a float too.

The following two lines print out texts illustrating the user about his or her new weights.
Holding for the User
The last expression holds for the user to click the Enter button:
raw_input("\n\nClick the enter button to exit.")

Chapter Three

Branching, Program Planning, and While Loops

U p to this point, the projects we have noted had incomprehensive, sequential direction, where every expression was implemented once each time. If for instance a person was restricted to just this category of programming, it could extremely hard (maybe if not possible) to write a complicated application. In this chapter, a person will be able to study the way to selectively allocate particular sections of his or her code and replicate each part of his or her Program. We will learn more, preferably the following in this chapter:

- How to develop random numbers while using *randrange()*

- How to apply *if* structures to run code based on a state of that code

- How to apply the *if-else* structures to create a choice based on a state or condition

- How to apply *if-else-elif* structures to develop an option based on several conditions or rules

- How to apply while loops to replicate sections of a person's Program

- How to Plan a person's your programs using *pseudocode*

Initiating the Guess My Number Game

In this chapter, the Program that an individual will develop is referred to as the classic number or digit guessing game. The game runs like this: the PC will choose any digit between 1 and 100 and the player role here will involve him or her attempts to guess it in some trials as possible. Every moment the player inserts or enters a guess, the PC briefs the player whether his or her estimate is too low or too high, or even on the right money. The moment the player guesses the digit, the game is over.

Generating Random Numbers

As long as the users need consistent, predictable outcomes from programs, in the most occasion are what causes the programs exciting in the user unpredictability: the expected change in the PC opponent's methodology or strategy, or an unknown creature reputing out from an erratic door. Random digits may distribute this component of surprise, and Python to offer a simple means to create those random digits or numbers.

Initiating Craps Roller Program

Craps Roller repeats what is known as the dice roll of the swift-paced, which is a casino game of craps. Here a person does not have to be aware of anything concerning craps to give thanks to the Program. Craps Roller main function is to prompt the role of two, six-sided dice, besides this, it also exhibits the value of every dice and their sum or total. To examine the dice values, the Program applies a function that creates random numbers. Here is an example of how the code looks like:

```
# Craps Roller
# Illustrate random number development # Michael Dawson - 12/29/02
import random
# develop random digit 1 - 6 die1 = random.randrange(6) + 1 die2 =
random.randrange(6) + 1
total = die1 + die2
print "A person rolled a", die1, "and a", die2, "for a total of", total
raw_input("\n\nClick the enter button to exit.")
```

Applying the import Statement or expression

The beginning line of code in the Program initiates the import expression. The Statement lets individuals load or import modules, in this instance, the random module in: *import random.*

Moreover, modules are documents that have code purposed to be applied to other programs. These modules always team together with a troupe of programming associated with a single region. The random module has a role associated with developing random digits and producing random outcomes. If a person ponders of his or her project as a developed program, then the modules are like unique toolkits that a person may pull out from the lock-up the moment that person requires them. But rather than going to the ledge and grasping a powered, round saw, here we have imported the random module for you. The moment you import a module, you may apply its code. Then, it just results in a matter of accessing it.

Accessing randrange()

The random module has a role, *randrange()*, which provides a random number without a decimal. The Craps Roller project accesses randrange() via the following role call: *random.randrange(6).* A person will realize that the Program does not directly call for the randrange(). But rather, it calls using the random.randrange(), since the project accesses randrange() via its module, random.

Conclusively, a person may request a function from an imported module by assigning giving the module a name or identity, then proceeded by a period, and then finally proceeded by the function calls itself. This strategy of Access is known as the dot notation. The dot notation is similar to the possessive noun in English. In English, "Nelson's Ferrari" signifies that Nelson owns the Ferrari. Applying dot notation, random.randrange() implies the function randrange() that is owned to the module random. Dot notation may be applied to ingress various components of the imported modules. At this juncture that we have known how to access randrange(), we would also need to be aware of how to apply it in Program.

Using randrange()

There are various means we can apply to call for the randrange(), but the easiest one is to apply a single, positive, integer argument. By applying this means, the function gets back to a random integer from and incorporating numbers from, 0, up to, but not incorporating, that digit. So the call random.randrange(6) provides either a 0, 1, 2, 3, 4, or 5. Alright, where's the 6? Well, randrange() is getting a random digit from a team of six numbers and the list of digits that begin with 0. A person can ponder this is odd, but he or she finds that most PC languages begin counting at 0 rather than 1. So, we have just added 1 to the outcome to access the correct values for a die:

die1 = random.randrange(6) + 1
Now, die1 gets either a 1, 2, 3, 4, 5, or 6.

Using the if Structure

Branching is an essential section of PC programming. This typically implies a person creating a conclusion to take a single direction or another. Via the *if* Structure, a Person's programs may branch to a part of the code or jump it, all based on the way a person set things up.

Initiating the Password Program

The Password program applies the *if* form to a sparking the login step of a highly guard PC server. The project grants the user ingress if he or she enters the right Password.

Here is the program code for Password:

```
# Password
# Illustrates the if structure # Michael Dawson - 12/29/02
print "Welcome to System Security Inc."
print "— where we secure our middle name\n."
password = raw_input("Enter your password: ") if password == "secret":
print "Access Granted."
raw_input("\n\nClick the enter button to exit.")
```

Examining the if Structure

The button to program Password is the if Structure: *if password == "secret": print "Access Granted"*. If the Structure is quite direct. A person may presumably find out what is taking place just by reading the code. If the Password is equivalent to "secret," then "Access Granted" is printed and the project continues to the following assertion. But, if it is not equivalent to "secret," the project does not print the information and proceeds directly to the following expression following the *if* structure.

Developing Conditions

All *if* structures contain a condition, which is defined as an expression or Statement or an assertion that is either true or false. Conditions are prevalent in our daily life, and we already familiar with them. For instance, the declaration "The temperature is 100 degrees outside." Can be regarded as a condition, which can either be It is either true or false. In the Password projection, the condition applied in the *if* Structure is Password == "secret." It implies that a password is equivalent to "secret." This condition calculates to either true or false, be contingent on the value of the Password. Most probably when the value if the value of the Password is equivalent to "secret," then the condition is correct, or otherwise, the condition would be stated false.

Understanding Comparison Operators

Conditions are commonly developed by juxtapose values. A person may contrast values using the comparison processor. We have already experienced one comparison processor by mean of the Password project. It' is the equivalent to comparison processor, always noted as ==.

The trap in this situation is equivalent-to comparison processors are two equal symbols in a row. Applying just a single same logo in a condition will bring in a syntax mistake since one equal sign represents there task processor. So, Password = "secret" is a task assertion. It allocates a value. And password == "secret" is a condition, which measures the value to either correct or false. Even though the task processor and the equal-to processor seem to be similar, they are two distinct things. The following example illustrates the summary of some comparison processor.

Operator	Meaning	Sample Condition	Evaluates To
1. ==	equal to	$5 == 5$	True
2. !=	not equal to	$8 != 5$	True
3. >	greater than	$3 > 10$	False
4. <	less than	$5 < 8$	True
5. >=	greater than or equal to	$5 >= 10$	False
6. <=	less than or equal to	$5 <= 5$	True

Applying comparison processors, a person may contrast any values. If he or she compares the strings, then he or she had obtained from the product based on the alphabetical order. For instance, "apple" < "orange" is correct since "apple" is alphabetically less than "orange."

Furthermore, Python permits an individual to contrast any values that he or she like, despite their category. But since a person can, it does not suggest that he or she should use the comparison operators. It is only useful to compare oranges to oranges and apples to apples, while also examining their values at the same category. Because a person may develop the condition "orange" < 2, it does not make much sense and "orange" < 2 is false if a person is curious.

Applying Indentation to Develop Blocks

A person can have realized that the second string of the *if* Structure, print "Access Granted," is indented. A block is referred to as one or more continuous lines indented by one element.

Blocks may be applied, among other means, as the final segment of an *if* Structure, which is identified as the expressions or team of expressions that obtains the accomplished *if* the condition is true. In the Password program, the block is the single statement print "AccessGranted." Besides blocks may be as many expressions as a person like, a person may append unique invite users who enter a proper password by converting the chunk in the *if* a structure like so:

> *if password == "secret": print "Access Granted"*
> *Print "Welcome! You must be someone who is much respected."*

Now, users who accurately enter a private password will perceive the Access Granted proceeded by Welcome! That person must be one who is highly respected. And if a user inserts or begins something besides the private Password, he or she would not see the two texts of true or false. In most occasions, indenting to develop blocks is not a choice. But rather stated as the only direction a person can take to define a block. In discussing Python, it is said to be one of the most known features of Python. We will contradict this saying and argue out that it is one of the controversial features on Python, will be elaborated in the following topics of discussion.

If for instances, you have ever programmed in another language other than Python language before, you will realize that odds indenting are always optional. Maybe a person could have noted each line of code flush left if he or she wanted to do so. Any indentation that is needed has its advantages since it builds consistency and readable code.

Building Your Own if Structure

To construct an if Structure, by apply if, then proceeded a condition, then a colon, and finally by a block of one or more expressions. If the

58

condition is enumerated to be accurate, then the feeling or statements that create the block are implemented. If the condition is measured to be false, then the project moves on to the following after the *if* structure.

Using the if-else Structure

Often a person will need his or her Program to "make an option" based on a condition: we need to perform one thing if the condition is correct, we need to offer something *else if* is false. The *if-else Structure* assigns a person with that power.

Initiating the Granted or Denied Program

The project Password performed a perfect job inviting a user who entered the right password, but it did not accomplish anything if the false Password was entered. Program Granted or Denied evaluates this issue by applying the *if-else Structure*. The next lines show off the brand-new and enhance the form.

Examining the else Statement

We only created a single change from the Password program. We attached an else clause to make an if-else structure:

> *if password == "secret": print "Access Permitted"*
> *else:*
> *print "Access Rejected."*

If the merit of the Password is equivalent to "secret," the project prints Access Permitted, just like it was done before. But now, we appreciate the else expression, the project prints Access Rejected otherwise. In an if-else structure, a person has warranted a single code block which will implement its roles. If the condition is accurate, then the block instantly proceeded, the condition is achieved.

If the condition is wrong, then the block promptly after the else is implemented. A person may develop an else clause instantly proceeding the if block with else, then followed by a colon, and finally followed by a block of expressions. The else expression must be in a similar block as its correlating if. The two-clause the if and else and if must be indented the in the same amount; or else, a person's program will develop a vile mistake.

Applying the if-elif-else Structure

Feasibility is the work of the if-elif-else Structure. It is one of the most robust and pliable of all the conditional structures that are available. It may be applied in different means, but appears in a quite handy way, when a person obtains a single variable that he or she needs to contrast to a bunch of varies values.

Initiating the Mood Computer Program

There was a broadly productive, fad product known as the Mood Ring In the mid-1970s. The ring divulges the wearer's mood via a color-converting gem. Well, the Mood PC project obtains the technology to the following stage by glancing into the vital force of the user and exhibiting his or her mood.

Okay, the project does not plum the emotional depths of the user via electro-dermal impulses transferred via the buttons. Rather than, the Mood PC develops a random digit to opt one of three faces to print via an if-elif-else structure. By the way, the Mood Ring did not reveal the wearer's emotions either. It was just an LCD that changed colors based on body temperature.

Examining the if-elif-else Structure

An if-elif-else structure could have an entire list of conditions for a project to calculate. In Mood Computer, the strings having distinct conditions would include:

- if mood == 0:

- Realize that you need to note the first condition applying an if clause, and then proceed by listing the rest of the conditions applying the elif.

- Elif clauses are built just like if clauses. And a person may contain as many as possible

- elif clauses as you like.

Creating While Loops

Loops are always around us, and you will also find that even a person's shampoo bottle contains looping specifications on them. This can look like an easy concept while another condition is correct, replicate something, but it's a robust piece of equipment in programming. It may come in a wholly handy, for instance, in creating a quiz to show the game. A person may need to alter his or her project: while there are quizzes left and continue playing the game. In a banking usage, a person may need to change his or her Program: while the user has not even entered a well-grounded account number, but continues asking the user for an account number. The *while loop* allows an individual to perform precisely this.

Initiating the Three-Year-Old Simulator Program

In the modern world today, many individuals do not access to spend the time they would like with their kids around their lives. An occupied teacher might be stuck at the school and notice his son at home who needs him or her. A salesperson may be busy on the road to realize his niece. Well, the Four-Year-Old Simulator gives solution to that issue by reproducing a conversation with a four-year-old kid. The aim to mimicking a four-year-old, it comes out, in the while loop.

As we may see here, the project continues to ask, Why? Until the response, Because. Is entered. The code for the Program is short:

```
# Four-Year-Old Simulator
# Illustrates the while loop # Michael Dawson - 1/3/03
print "\tWelcome to the 'Four-Year-Old Simulator'\n."
print "This project simulates a conversation with a four-year-old kid."
print "Try to stop
the madness.\n."
reply = ""
while reply != "Because.": reply = raw_input("Why?\n")
Print "Oh. Okay."
raw_input("\n\nClick the enter button to exit.")
```

Examining the while Structure

The loop from the Four-Year-Old Simulator project has just two lines:
while response != "Because.":reply = raw_input("Why? ")

If the Structure of the while loop appears known to us, there would be a better reason, which bears a conspicuous similarity to its relative, the if structure. The only distinction here is that if is substituted by while. And the resemblances are not just skin-deep. In both formats, if the condition is correct, the block, which often called the loop body in a loop, is implemented. But in the while format, the PC measures the condition and implements the block over and over again, not until the condition is wrong. This is perhaps the reason it is called a loop.

Initializing the Sentry Variable

Generally, *'the while loops'* are always managed by a look-out variable, a variable applied in the condition and contrasted to some other merits. Like a human guard, a person may ponder of his or her guard variable as a watch, aiding form a disturbance around the while loop's block. In the Four-Year-Old Simulator project, the watch variable is replied. It is applied in the condition and is contrasted to the line "Because." before the chunk is implemented every time. It is, therefore, essential to introduce the entry of a person's variable. In most occasions, the guard variables are introduced right before the loop itself. That is what we did:

```
reply = ""
while reply != "Because.": reply = raw_input("Why? ")
```

Note that the trap here is that if the guard variable does not contain a value the moment the condition is equal, a person's project will create a mistake. It is always a better concept to initialize a person's sentry variables to some category of an empty value. I allocate ", the empty string, to reply. While we can allocate the string "aardvark," and the project can toil just in a similar way, it can create the code needlessly confusing.

Checking the Sentry Variable

A person is required to make sure that it is viable for the while condition to calculate to accuracy at some point; otherwise, the chunk will never operate. Take, for instance, a single minor change to the loop you have been working with:

> reply = "Because."
> while reply != "Because.": reply = raw_input("Why? ")

Because the reply is equivalent to "Because." right before the loop, the block will never operate. The project will behave like the loop is not even in that place.

Updating the Sentry Variables

Once a person has instituted his or her condition, he or she would need to introduce the sentry variable, and make sure that under the similar conditions the loop block will operate quite well, through this that person would have a functioning loop. Next, that person also needs to ensure that the loop will end. If a person, for instance, notes a loop that not in any circumstances ends, then he or she would realize that they have generated a continual loop. At any given moment or another, all that programmers have always generated fortuitously is an infinite loop and observed their projects becoming stuck while performing some task over and over. Or even observe their projects just as unpretentious freeze up. An example of an eternal loop would include:

> counter = 0
> while counter <= 10 print counter

What the user of the program implied was for the loop to print the digits from 0 to 10. Woefully, what this program performs is print 0, forever. The programmer could not recall how to alter counter, the sentry variable that is on the inner region of the block. What is essential for us to recall here is that the values in the condition must be altered on the inner side of the loop block. For instance, it is argued that if these values never alter, then the loop will also never stop or end, and that person contains an eternal loop.

Avoiding Infinite Loops

A single category of the interminable loop is in the situation where the sentry variable is not in any chance updated like it was observed in the previous explanation. But there are many covert types of the never-stopping loop. If you check on the proceeding program, you will affirm that the never-stopping loop does change the value of the sentry variable in the loop structure. There might be a problem here since loops never end.

Initiating the Losing Battle Program

The Losing Battle program is said to be describing the final, courageous fight of a paladin dazzling by an array of trolls, a situation one may find in a role-running game. The project describes the fight action. It narrates the scuffle, blow-by-blow, as the paladin conquers a troll, but then obtains much destruction. In the final, the program usually terminates with the death of the paladin. Or performs it? Here is an example of such code:

```
# Losing Battle
# Illustrates the dreaded interminable loop # Michael Dawson - 1/2/03
print "Your lone paladin is encircled by a huge horde of trolls."
print "Their deteriorating green bodies which are extended and melting
into the horizon."
```

```
print "Your paladin unsheathes his sword and starts the final battle of his
life.\n."
health = 10
trolls = 0
destroyed = 3
while health != 0: trolls += 1
health = health – destroyed
print "Your paladin swings and conquers an evil troll, " \ "but obtains,"
damage,
"damage points.\n."
print "Your paladin battled valorously and conquered," trolls, "trolls."
print "But alas,
your paladin is no more."
raw_input("\n\nClick the enter button to exit.")
```

Tracing the Program

Well, it may appear like the project contains a cogent mistake. A perfect mean to track down this type of mistake is to discover a person program's execution. Tracing would imply that a person simulating the operating of his or her and perform exactly what it would perform, each order keeping track of the values allocated to variables. Through this mean, a person can step via the project, scrutinize exactly what is occurring at every point, and trace the state of condition that connives to result to the bug in a person's code. The most fundamental means to discover a program is with archaic paper and pencil. We were able to develop columns, one for every condition and variable. So before starting this page, it may appear like this:

health   trolls   destroy health != 0

Right after the condition of the *while form* is calculated, the page may appear like this:

health	trolls	destroy	health != 0
10	0	4	accurate

The moment the condition is said to be accurate, the loop accomplishes for the first time. After a single entire time via and back up to assess the worth of the condition once more, my discover may appear like this:

health	trolls	destroy	health != 0
10	0	4	accurate
7	1	4	accurate

After sometimes via the loop, the trace may appear like this:

health	trolls	destroy	health != 0
10	0	4	accurate
7	1	4	accurate
4	2	4	accurate
1	3	4	accurate
-2	4	4	accurate

health	trolls	destroy	health != 0
-5	5	4	accurate
-7	6	4	accurate

The trace had to be stopped since it seemed like it was in an infinite loop. Because the merit of health is (-) negative and not equivalent to 0 in the three concluding strings of the trace, the condition is stated to accurate. The issue here is, health will at no time become 0. It would just develop in the negative (-) direction every moment the loop prosecutes. As an outcome, the condition will not at any time become wrong or false, and the loop will at no time stop.

Creating Conditions that Can Become False

Besides ensuring that merit in a while loop's condition convert, a person should make sure that the condition can finally assess to false or wrong; or else, a person can still have an infinite loop on a person's hands. In the instance of the Losing Battle project, the fix is simple. The string with the condition requires to becoming while health > 0: In case, the health becomes 0 or even negative, the condition assesses to false, and the loop concludes. To be sure of this, a person can track the program utilizing this brand-new condition:

Health		trolls	destroy	health > 0
10	0	4		accurate
7	1	4		accurate
4	2	4		accurate
1	3	4		accurate
-2	4	4		false

Treating Values as Conditions

If instance you are required to evaluate 35 + 2 the most straightforward answer you can give is swiftly 37. But if you needed to assess 37 as either being correct or wrong, you will presumably provide an, "Huh?" But the concept of searching at any value as either being accurate or inaccurate is valid in Python. Any merit, of any form, may be treated in this manner. So, 2749, 8.6, " mango," 0, and "" can each be analyzed as being correct or incorrect. This can appear to be bizarre, but it is always simple, as the laws that establish them as being accurate and inaccurate are relaxed. More crucially, analyzing values in this means may create for many more effective conditions.

Initiating the Maitre D' Program

If a person has not rebuffed at a fancy, a French hotel lately, then this program is just for you. Maitre D' invites peoples to the splendid eatery and then asks them how much money they slip to their host. If those people you provide zero dollars, and then those people are rightly disregarded. If a person offers some other amount, then their table would be waiting. From observing a program running, a person may not be happy. This may look like something a person has already performed. The distinction would be that there is no comparison processor applied in this program. Rather, the amount of money is regarded as a condition. You may observe the code and see the way it functions:

```
# Maitre D'
# Illustrates treating a value as a condition # Michael Dawson - 1/3/03
print "Invite to the Chateau D' Food."
print "It appears we are wholly full this evening. \n."
 money = int(raw_input("How many dollars does a person slip the
Maitre D'? "))
if money:
Print "Ah, I am jogged to recall a table. Right this direction." otherwise:
Print "Please, sit. It might be a while." raw_input("\n\nClick the enter
button to exit.")
```

Analyzing Any Value as either being True or False

The new idea is illustrated in the line:

a) if money:

You will realize that the money is not collated to any other value. Money is the condition. The moment it comes to assessing digits, 0 is wrong, and everything else is correct or accurate. This would imply that the above string is equal to

b) if money != 0:

The initiate version is easier, more modish, and more intuitive. It scrutinizes more naturally and may be translated to "if there is money." The laws for what creates a value correct or incorrect are natural. The fundamental principle is this: any desolate or zero value is incorrect; everything else is considered right. So, 0 assess to false, but any other value determines to true. The empty line, ", is incorrect, while any separate line is correct. As a person may see, almost every amount is right. It is only the desolate or zero merits that is accurate. He or she will find that testing for a forlorn number is a general thing that one can perform, so this manner of treating numbers may come up a lot in projects. Eventually, to write here is that if a person enters a negative (-) dollar value, the maitre d' would still seat him or her. That persons need to recall, for digits, only 0 is accurate. This may imply that all the negative values are correct, this would be similar to the positive ones

Developing Intentional Infinite Loops

Coming soon after the part known as Avoiding Infinite Loops, in which a person may be more than amazed to see a segment about developing infinite loops. Are not infinite loops usually an error? Well, if a loop were accurately unlimited, that is, it can at no time end, and then yes, it would be a reasonable mistake. But what we call purpose unlimited loops are an unlimited curve with an egress condition constructed into the loop structure. The perfect means in which a person can understand a purposeful unlimited curve is to look at a sample.

Initiating the Finicky Counter Program

The Finicky Counter program can tally from 1 to 10, applying an intentional unlimited loop. It is finicky since it does not like the digit 5 and jumps it. The following are examples of codes to this program:
 # Finicky Computes
 # Illustrates the break and constant assertion # Michael Dawson - 1/3/03
count = 0 while Accurate:
count += 1
 # end loop if the count is greater than 10 if count > 10:
break # jump 5
if count == 5: constant
print count
raw_input("\n\nClick the enter button to exit.")

Understanding True and False

A person may realize that any merit may be analyzed as accurate or correct or wrong or inaccurate, but Python also contains a direct mean to represent these values. A person may apply them in a condition or even allocate them to a variable. Here it shall be illustrated that a person may require what he or she mean via an informative session.

>> if Accurate or True:
print "I'm true or accurate!"
I'm true!

Since True is true, the if block implements and prints the string "I'm true!"

>> game_over = Accurate
>> if game_over:
print "Sorry, your game is over."
Sorry, a person's game is over.

Since game_over is equivalent to True, the if block implements and prints the string "Sorry, a person's game is over."

>> if False: else:
print "I'm true!" print "I'm false!"
I'm false!

Applying the break Assertion to Exit a Loop

Here we put the loop with:

while True:

This technology may imply that the loop will proceed forever, except if there is an exit condition in the loop structure. Luckily, this may be put in one:

end loop if compute greater than 10 if count > 10:
break

Because the count is enhanced by one every moment the loop structure starts, it will finally stretch 11. When it performs, the break assertion, this may imply that "flare-up of the loop," is implemented and the loop terminates.

Applying the continue Assertion to skip Back to the Top of a Loop

Before the count is printed, we incorporated the lines below:

> *# jump 5*
> *if count == 5: continue*

The continue assertion implies we skip back to the top of the loop. The *"while condition"* is measured at the top of the curve, and the loop is entered to check if it is accurate. So the moment count is equivalent to 5, the project does not attain to the print count assertion. But instead it gets right back to the top of the curve, and five is jumped and in most times never printed.

Understanding When to Use break and continue

A person may apply a break and carry on with any loop he or she generates. There are not constrained for use in purposefully limited loops. But sometimes they should be applied sparingly. It is said that both continue and break it difficult for anyone to perceive the flow of a loop and analyze it under what state it ends. Besides a person do not need to cut and continue. Any loop a person may not apply them may be noted without them. In Python, there are moments when an intentional unlimited loop may be explicit than a traditional loop when compared. In those few instances where it is clunky to note the loop with the reasonable condition, some programmers may prefer applying intentional unlimited loop. But once more we said earlier that if possible, a person should try to avoid them with all means since they make work cumbersome.

Applying Compound Conditions

Up to this juncture, we have been able to illustrate only the comparison where two values are incorporated. This is what is known in most cases, as a natural or straightforward condition. This is presumably what is known as the most general means to generate a condition. In most cases, people may find themselves hoping for a more robust niche of the condition. With high expectation, a person can put together this simple or easy condition to become compound conditions. Applying compound conditions, a person program may develop conclusions that are fundamentally based on how teams of values compared.

Initiating the Exclusive Network Program

Particular groups are no joke unless a person is a member. So, I developed the Exclusive Network project. It triggers an elite PC connection in the place only where one can pick some numbers. The membership entails some few top game designers who are known globally today ad this would not be a bad company. Just like in the actual world computer system that every individual contains to enter a user name and a password. A member is obliged to enter their password and username, without performing this that member would not be in a position to log in to his or her computer. For a login to be successful, the member is personally being welcomed by being greeted. This also applies in the real world system where each has a security measurement to protect their accounts from being invaded by the wrong people.

Since we are not elitist, visitors are permitted to log in, since they have the minimum security level, though. Here is an example of how this code may look like:

```
# Exclusive Network
# Illustrates logical operators conditions # Michael Dawson - 1/3/03
print "\tExclusive PC Network" print "\t\tMembers only!\n"
security = 0 username = ""
while not username:
username = raw_input("Username: ")
password = ""
while not password:
password = raw_input("Password: ")
if username == "M.Dawson" and password == "secret": print "Hi,
Mike."
security = 5
elif username == "S.Meier" and password == "civilization": print "Hey,
Sid."
security = 3
elif username == "S.Miyamoto" and password == "mariobros": print
"What's up, Shigeru?"
security = 3
elif username == "W.Wright" and password == "thesims": print "How
goes it, Will?"
security = 3
elif username == "guest" or password == "guest": print "Welcome,
guest."
security = 1 else:
print "Login not processed. A person may not be so exclusive.\n"
raw_input("\n\nClick the enter button to exit.")
```

Understanding the 'not' Logical Operator

In this topic, our main purpose is to ensure that the programmer gets something for the password and username because only pushing the Enter button which upshot in the desolate string, would not perform successfully. Therefore, we need a loop that cannot ask for a username until the user enters something. This is the curve or loop we came up with for obtaining the username:

```
username = ""
while not username:
    username = raw_input("Username: ")
```

In this case, we were able to apply the logical not processor in a while condition. It functions a little more like the statement "not." In the English language, obtaining the statement "not" ahead of something which generates a new phrase that implies the opposite of the old one. In Python, placing not ahead of a condition makes a brand-new condition that assesses to the inverse of the old one. That implies not a username is accurate in the moment username is incorrect. And not username is inaccurate when the username is genuine. There is also another way how it doesn't work:

username,	not the username
true	false
false	true

Because the username is accepted to the desolate line in the project, it starts as inaccurate or false. That makes not username accurate, and the loop operates the first time. Then, the project becomes merit for username from the user. If the programmer pushes Enter, the username is the empty line, just as before. And as illustrated earlier, not username is accurate, and the loop gets operating. So, provided that the programmer presses Enter, the loop continues running, and the programmer continues obtaining induced for a username. But the moment the programmer eventually enters any things, username gets a brand-new line, other things other than the desolate string. That causes the username to assess to accurate and not username determine to inaccurate. As an outcome, the loop stops, just like we needed. Thus, the project performs a similar thing for variable security.

Understanding the 'and' Logical Operator

If a member needs to log in to this exclusive connection, the member must enter a username and the security that is realized in conjunction. If for instances, Sid Meier needs to log in, he obliged to enter S.Meier for his username and progress for his security. If Sid does not enter both, just that means, he cannot log in. S.Meier and Mario bros would not function. Either will M.Dawson and progress. The union progress and S.Meier fail too. The project searches that Sid enters S.Meier for his username and progress for his password with the proceeding code:

elif username == "S.Meier" and password == "progress":

The string has one compound condition composed of two calm conditions. The easy states are username == "S.Meier" together with password == "progress". These are just like the states or conditions a person have already seen, but they contain been combined by the and reasonable processor to build an extensive, compound state, username == "S.Meier" and password == "progress." This compound state, though extended than a person applied to, is still just a state, that implies that it may be neither be accurate nor inaccurate. So, the moment the username == "S.Meier" and password == "progress" accurate, and the same moment it is inaccurate? Well, just like in the English language, "and" may imply to both sayings. So, the state is accurate only if both username == "S.Meier" and password == "progress" is accurate; or else it is inaccurate.

The project, of course, functions for others apart from Sid Meier. Via an if-elif-else form, the project searches four distinct username and password sets. If programmers get to access a realize a set, the member is personally invited and allocated a password value.

Understanding the 'or' Logical Processor

Visitors are permitted in the system, too, but with a limited security level. To make it easy for a guest to attempt the system, all he or she has to perform is enter visitor for neither the username nor password. The proceeding lines of code log in a visitor:

```
"visitor" or password == elif username == "visitor": print "Welcome, victor."
security = 1
```

The elif state, username == "visitor" or password == "visitor," appears in mostly like the other conditions, like those applied for the members. But there would be a core distinction. The visitor condition is developed by applying the logic or processor. A compound condition developed with an operator is accurately provided that at least one of the more accessible states is accurate. Besides, the processor functions like in the English Language.

Condition is accurate.

In this certain instance, if username == "visitor" is accurate or if password == "visitor" is accurate, or even if both are even accurate, then username == "visitor" or password == "visitor" is accurate; or else, it's inaccurate. Here is another mean to see at how or functions:

password == "visitors"== username == "visitors" or password == "visitors" username == "visitors"

accurate	*accurate*	*accurate*
accurate	*inaccurate*	*accurate*
inaccurate	*accurate*	*accurate*
Inaccurate	*inaccurate*	*inaccurate*

Planning Your Programs

Up to this point, all the projects we have been able to illustrate in this chapter have been the easiest ones. The concept of programming any of them appears like overkill. Programming a person's, even the minimal ones, will nearly usually result in time that is always frustration stored. Planning is more similar to construction. For instance, a person can envisage a contractor constructing a building for another person a blueprint. Yikes! He or she might be capable of stopping up with a structure that contains around 12 bathrooms, no windows, and an entrance on the second floor of the building. The total cost of the whole building maybe 10 time more than its estimated price. Programming may also adopt the same model; without a plan, a person will struggle through the process, dissipating time. A person may even result in a project that does not require quite an activity. Program designing is so essential that there is a whole region of software engineering devoted to it. But even a starting user may gain from a few easy designing pieces of equipment and proficiency.

Developing Algorithms with Pseudocode

An algorithm is defined as a pair of a set of explicit, simple-to-follow specifications for completing some assignment. It is more like a draft for a person's program. It is an activity that a person must plan out first before planning, to direct him or her along as he or she codes. An algorithm is not just an objective; it is a solid list of procedures that one should adhere to. So, for instance, "Be a Trillionaire" may not be described as an algorithm. It looks more like what one would like to achieve.

Moreover, algorithms are usually noted in pseudocode, which mostly falls in between English and a programming language. For anyone who knows the English language may also be in a position to analyze the algorithm. At the same moment, the algorithm should discern indistinct like a program. The first four strings bear a resemblance of an if-else structure, which is intentional.

Applying Stepwise Refinement to Your Algorithms

Like any other plan out there, a person's algorithm may not be completed after just a simple single draft. Usually, algorithms require various approvals before they may be executed in the code. Stepwise classification, or refinement, is one of the operations applied to rewrite algorithms so that they became prepared for execution. Stepwise refinement is quite natural because it typically implies as to make it more detailed. By following every procedure in an algorithm and cracking it down into a series of more straightforward methods, the algorithm becomes nearer to programming code. In stepwise classification or refinement, a person stores would be cracking down.

Returning to the Guess My Number Game

The Guess My Number game joins various many of the ideas that a person would be studying in this particular topic. But, more fundamentally, it stands for the entire initial match that a person may apply to bluster to his or her pals, relatives, or even to the members of the opposite sex.

Planning the Program

To planner design the game, a person may be required to note down first some pseudocode:

select a random digit
while the player has not guessed the number, you need to allow the player guess
applaud the player

This would not be the first bad pass, but it would be missing some crucial components. In the first instant, the program is supposed to discern the player if the guess is on its maximum or minimum. In the second instance, the program should be able to keep account of how many guesses the player has created and then show the player this digit when the game is concluded.

The crucial hint here will be if a person's first project design is not accomplished. Beginning from the planning of the core concept first, then fill in space until it is done.

Here is an example of refinement of an algorithm:

welcome the player first to the game and then elaborate more
it selects a random digit in between 1 and 100
urge the player for a guess
place the digit of guesses to 1
while the player's guess is not equivalent the
digit if the guess is higher than the digit
appraise the player to guess lower or else

notify the player to guess a higher number to attain a new guess from the player

raise the digit of guesses by 1

applaud the player on guessing the digit

allow the player to realize how many guesses it took

After performing these, all a person can be confident to now write the project since he or she will be feeling ready to do so. After doing this, you will need to take a look over the few proceeding sections and have a look at how directly pseudocode may sometimes translate into Python.

Developing the introduction Comment Block

You need to look at all programs to see all the good ones. All suitable programs will always start with a block of comments, which is still describing the program's objective and clarifying its author:

 # You can try to Guess My Digit

#

 # The PC selects a random digit in between number 1 and 100 # The player attempts to guess it, and the PC allows him or her to do so

 # the player realizes if the guess maybe is too high, or even too low # or right on the money

#

 # Michael Dawson - 1/8/03

Importing the random Module

To make it more fun, the program requires to create a random digit. So, to make this possible, we introduced the random module: *import random*

Explaining the Game

The game might be quite easy, but you may be required to give a little bit of elaboration which would not hurt you anyway:

print "\tWelcome to 'Guess My Digit'!"
print "\nI'm pondering of a digit or value between 1 and 100." print "Try to guess it in as few trials as possible.\n."

Setting the Initial Values

Next, we were able to set all the variables into their initial values:

 # set the initial numbers
the_digit = random.randrange(100) + 1 guess = int(raw_input("Take a guess: ")) attempts = 1

Therefore, the_digit stands for the value the player has to guess. We allocate it a random integer which can be between 1 to 100 with a call to random.randrange(). Next, raw_input() gives the player's first guess. int() changes the guess to an integer. We then allocate this value to guess. We assign attempts, which could stand for the digit of the guesses so far, the number

Developing a Guessing Loop

Designing or creating a guessing loop is said to be the necessary thing in a program. The loop has the role of implementing provided that the player has not accurately guessed the PC's digit or number. During the looping process, the player's guess is contrasted to the PC's digit. If the guess comes out to be higher than the digit, Lower. . . is printed; or else, Higher. . . is printed. The player gets into the next guess, and the digit of guesses counter is increased.

```
# guessing loop
while (guess != the_digit):
if (guess > the_digit): print "Lower..."
otherwise:
print "Higher..."
guess = int(raw_input("Take a guess: ")) attempts += 1
```

Congratulating the Player

The moment the player guesses the digit right, the guess is equivalent to the_digit, which implies that the loop condition;

- *Guess!= the_digit, is inaccurate, and the loop concludes. At that situation, the player may always require to be applauded:*

- *Print ", An individual, guessed it! The value or number was", the_number print "And it only got that individual," attempts, "attempts! \n"*

The PC notifies the player in most situations what the private or secret value or number was and the attempts the number to the player to guess.

Waiting for the Player to Quit

As usually, the concluding line holds back tolerantly for the player to pushes the Enter button: *raw_input("\n\nClick the enter button to exit.")*

Chapter Four

Loops, Tuples, and Strings:
The Word Jumble Game

In the previous chapter, you have gained knowledge on how variables are essential means of obtaining data, but as a person's programs develop in size and complexity so that the digit of a person's variables can keep track of all of them. Thus, in this section, we will be able to study mostly about the concept of patterns and achieve new form known as the tuple, which allows a person to plan and handle data in ordered groups. Here in this chapter, a person will also be able to see how a category they have already come across, the string, is a pattern or sequence too. We shall also be in a position to learn about a new type of loop that is constructed just to work with designs. Notably, we will be able to study the way a person can perform them. In this chapter, we will focus on the following:

- How to build for loops to move via a sequence

- How one can apply the *range() function* to develop a pattern of digits that would

- We shall also learn about how to treat strings as sequences (patterns)

- We will also learn how to apply tuples to harness the strength of the pattern.

- We shall also learn how people can apply sequence roles and processors in their works

- Finally, we shall learn about Index and slice patterns or sequences

Initiating the Word Jumble Game

The Word Jumble game uses various new concepts as we shall see later in this chapter. The Word Jumble Game re-generates the core word jumble that an individual may find in the Sunday paper since we all know these were the things that people applied in the ancient times before the innovation of the internet. The PC only selects a random statement from a team and the develop a jumbled form of it, where the letters are situated in a random sequence. The player here will have to guess the first word to come out as a win in this jumble game.

Using for Loops

In the previous chapter, we were able to learn about a particular type of loop known as *the while loop*, which we said duplicates a section of a person's code based on a condition. This duplication of the while loop is only possible as long as its condition is accurate, where some codes will have to duplicate. The *for loop* also reproduces as a section of a program based on a pattern. For instance, if a person has ever noted a list of his or her 10 best movies, then probably he or she have created a form of sequence which they don't even know they have done.

Additionally, A for loop duplicates its loop structure for every component of the pattern or sequence, in order. The moment it gets to the end of the pattern, the loop stops. As a sample, a person may prefer his or her list of sequence once more. A for loop may pass via this order of movie heads, one after the other, and then print each one of them. But the recommended way to analyze a *for loop* is to observe one of it in action.

Initiating the Loopy String Program

This project obtains a statement from the programmer and prints it in the form of letters so that it can be in a position to isolate different lines. This uncomplicated program offers a better example of a *for a loop*. The following are some examples of the code:

```
# Loopy String
# Illustrate the for loop with a string # Michael Dawson - 1/26/03
word = raw_input("Enter a word: ")s
print "\nHere's every letter in a person's word:" for a letter in the word:
print letter
raw_input("\n\nClick the enter button to exit.")
```

Understanding for Loops

The new concept in this project is the *for loop*, which is just the presented in the next two brief lines: *for a letter in the word: print letter*. Even before a person realizes any issue concerning the *for loops*, the code is quite explicit. But in this chapter, it will be discussed how they function. It is proven that any string that one may enter is a sequence such as "Loop."

All patterns or sequences are compost of component. For strings, every part is unique nature. In this instance, the fundamental unit is the character illustrated as "L" the second nature is "o," and so on. Because a *for loop* runs via a sequence on a single unit at a time, this loop runs via the letters in "Loop" one after the other. To commence in this section, the letter attains the first structure in word, which is presented as "L." Then, the loop structure, that is the print assertion, exhibits L. Then, letter attains the proceeding character in a word, which is illustrated as "o." The PC shows o, and the loop keeps on until every character in the string "Loop" is exhibited.

Developing a for Loop

To generate a *for loop*, a person may adhere to the sample in the program. Should begin with for, then proceed by a variable for every component, then followed by in, advanced by the pattern that a person needs to loop via, next by a colon, and then finally, followed by the loop structure.

Counting with a for Loop

The moment a person notes a program, he or she will always find that he or she wants to count. And *for loops* is still the recommended direction to take. In coalition with the *for loop*, a person is recommended to use the Python's *range() function* to compute in all sorts of means.

Initiating the Counter Program

The Counter program illustrates to people the way they can apply the *range() function* to develop lists of digits. Matched with a *for loop*, people can always apply the list to compute onward or reverse, or even to jump digits if they like. The following are how the code for the program may look like:

```
# Counter
# Illustrates the range() function # Michael Dawson - 1/26/03
print "Computing:" for i in range(10):
```

88

print i,

print "\n\nComputing by fives:" for i in range(0, 50, 5):

print i,

print "\n\nComputing onwards:" for i in range(10, 0, -1):

print i,

raw_input("\n\nClick the enter button to exit.\n")

Counting Forwards

The initial loop in the project computes onwards as illustrated below:

for i in range(10): print i,

This for loop functions in the same way as the *for loop* that was illustrated in the Loopy String program, where it loops via a pattern. It might be difficult hard to point out what the sequence looks like. The sequence or pattern of the loop passes via the *developed range()* *function*. It then generates a sequence of digits, that give *a range()* a positive integer and generates a sequence commencing with 0, up to, but not incorporating, the digit a person assigned before. Have a look at a section of an informative session that we were able to operate with IDLE:

>> range(7) [0, 1, 2, 3, 4,5,6]

>> range(12)

[0, 1, 2, 3, 4, 5, 6, 7, 8, 9, 10, 11]

Another means that a person can use to look at this loop is to replace the outcomes of the *range() function* into the code the moment a person peruse it. Thus a person can assume that it peruses:

for i in [0, 1, 2, 3, 4, 5, 6, 7, 8, 9,10,11]:

print i,

89

And that the *range() function* call is substituted with the pattern of digits that it generates. This loop is a correct one, as a person may develop a list of numbers by bounding them in parenthesis that is isolated by the use of commas. But they do not run off by developing a bunch of lists. More information about these lists will be discussed later.

Counting by Fives

The proceeding loop counts by fives: *for i in range(0, 70, 5): print i.* It performs by using *range()* that develops a list of digits that are multiples of 5. To generate a pattern of digits with *range()*, a person may assign it the beginning point, the stop point, and then finally the value by which to compute. Here, the pattern begins at 0, and jumps to 5 every time, too, but not involving, 70. That was applied in the interactive mode once more so that a person may perceive the actual pattern range(0, 70, 5) produces:

>> *range(0, 70, 5)*
[0, 5, 10, 15, 20, 25, 30, 35, 40, 45, 50, 55, 60, 65]

You may realize that though the pattern or sequence stops at 65. You need to recall that 70 is the stop point, so it is not incorporated. If a person needed to incorporate 70, his or her stop point has to be greater than 70. So, range(0, 71, 5) would do the trick.

Counting Backwards

The previous loop in the program counts in reverses:

for i in range(20, 0, -1): print i,

It carries this since the previous digit in the *range()* call is -1. This shows that the function runs from the beginning point to the stop point by appending -1 every time. This is similar to saying, "take away 1." Once more, the stop point is not incorporated, so the loop computes from 20 down to 1 and does not incorporate 0.

Applying Sequence/pattern Operators and Functions with Strings

As we have discussed before, strings are just a single form of a pattern, compost by individual natures. Python provides some essential roles and processors that function with any pattern, incorporating strings. These processors and functions can notify a person some fundamental but also illustrate some crucial things concerning a pattern or sequence, like how long it is or whether a particular unit is in it.

Initiating the Message Analyzer Program

This proceeding program understands any text that a person enters. It may illustrate to that person how extended the information is and whether or not it has the most general letter in the English language (the letter "e"). The project completes this with a brand-new pattern role and pattern processor. This project applies the *len() function* and the in the processor to result in some data about a person's message. Below is how some of the code for the program:

```
# Message or Text Analyzer
# Illustrates the len() function and the in processor # Michael Dawson -
1/26/03
text = raw_input("Enter a message: ")
print "\nThe length of a person's text or message is:," len(text or
message)
```

91

print "\nThe most general letter in the English language, 'e,,'" if "e" in
text or message:
print "is in a person's text or message." else:
print "is not in a person's text or message.
" raw_input("\n\nPress the enter key to exit.")

Applying the len() Function

The moments after the project ships in the random module and reaches the user's text; it prints the text length with: *print "\nThe length of a person's text or message is:," len(text or message)*. A person may give any pattern that he or she desires to len(), and it will notify that person that pattern's length. A pattern's length is the digit of units it is compost of in its structure. Because the text contains 10 characters in it a person may compute each nature, incorporating the space and the exclamation point, it contains a length of about 10, just like the PC would illustrate to a person.

Applying the in Operator

The letter "e" is the most often letter used in the English language. The program utilizes the proceeding strings to measure whether "e" is in the text the programmer entered:

print "\nThe most often letter used in the English language, 'e,'" if "e" in
text or message:
print "is in a person's text or message." otherwise:
print "is not in a person's text or message."

The condition if the expression is "e" in text or message. If the message keeps the character "e," it is accurate. If the text does not have "e," then it is inaccurate. In the example run, the number of text is "Game Over!", which have the character "e." So, the condition "e" in-text assessed to accurate and the PC printed "is in a person's message." If the condition had been inaccurate, then the PC may contain the display which is not in a personal text. If a component is in a pattern, it is said to be a group of the pattern. A person may apply in anywhere in his or her programs to confirm if a component is a member of pattern or sequence. Just set the unit you desire to verify for, proceeded by in, and then followed by the pattern. This generates a condition. If the component is a member, the condition is accurate; else it is inaccurate.

Indexing Strings

By applying a *for loop*, a person would be able to run via a string, a single character at a time, in that order. This is referred to as sequential ingress, which implies that a person may have to go via pattern one unit after the other, begging from the starting point. Sequential intrusion is like running via a stack of sturdy boxes that a person may only lift a single one at a time. To reach to the bottom box in a heap of five, he or she would have to raise the top box, then proceed to the other box, followed by the other box, until he or she reaches the final box.

It would be perfect for taking the last box directly without interruption with the others. This sort of direct ingress is known as random access. Random intrusion or access permits a person to reach any component in a pattern directly. Fortunately, there would be another means where we can randomly get components of a pattern. This is known as indexing. Via indexing, a person can categorize a place or index of a digit in a pattern and attain the unit at that position. In the box sample, a person may obtain the bottom box directly, by inquiring for box digit or number five.

Initiating the Random Access Program

The Random Access program applies the pattern indexing to ingress random forms in a string directly. The project selects a random place from the string "index," and then prints the letter and the position digit. The program operates this 10 times to offer a perfect example of random positions. The proceeding is the code for the program:

```
# Random Access
# Illustrates string indexing # Michael Dawson - 1/27/03
Ship in random word = "index."
print "The word is:," word, "\n."
high = len(word) low = -len(word) for i in range(10):
position = random.randrange(low, high)
print "word[", position, "]\t", word[position]
raw_input("\n\nClick the enter button to exit.")
```

Working with Positive Position Numbers

In this project, one of the tasks that we performed was to allocate a string number to a variable:

```
word = "index"
```

Nothing appears new here. But by carrying out this, we can develop a pattern like each time we developed a string, where every nature has a numbered position. The starting letter being, "i," is at position 0. We need to recall that the PCs always begin computing from 0. The second letter would be, "n," is at position 1. Then the third, "d," position at 2, and proceeds on. Accessing the personal nature of a string is straightforward. To ingress the letter in position 0 from the variable assertion, a person would just write the word [0]. For any other area, that same person would need only to replace that number. To aid him or her cement the concept, have a look at a section of a communicative session we had before:

Working with Negative Position Numbers

Except for the concept that the initial letter of a string is at position 0 and not 1, toiling with positive position digits may appear quite natural. But there is also a mean to get units of a pattern via a negative position digit. With positive position values, a person may point of reference is the starting of the pattern. For strings, this would imply that the initial letter is where a person may begin counting. But with the negative position values or numbers, a person can commence counting from the end. For strings, that implies them to begin counting from the concluding letter and toil in reverse. The perfect way one can understand how the negative position digits function is to look at an example. Have a look at another communicative session we had before, using the string "index":

```
>> word = "index"
>> print word[-1] 'x'
>> print word[-2] 'e'
>> print word[-3] 'd'
>> print word[-4] 'n'
>> print word[-5] 'i'
```

A person may perceive this from this session that word[-1] ingresses the final letter of "index", the "x." the moment he or she applies a negative position digits, -1 would imply that the last number is an element, the index -2 means that the second to the final item, the index -3 indicates the third to the previous unit, and so on. Sometimes it creates a lot of sense for a person's reference point to be at the end of a pattern.

```
>> word = "index"
>> print word[0] i
>> print word[1] n
>> print word[2] d
>> print word[3] e
>> print word[4] x
```

Accessing a Random String Element

It is the moment to return to the Random Access program. To ingress a random letter from the "index," we need to create random digits. So, the first thing that we had to do in the program was to ship in the random module: *import random*

Next, we needed a mean in which we could select any valid position value in word, which would be either positive or negative. We needed our program to be in a position to create a random value between -5 and 4, inclusive since those numbers are possible position numbers of the word. On an added advantage, the *random.randrange()* function may take two concluding points and result in a random value between them. So, we decided to generate two endpoints as illustrated below: *high = len(word) low = -len(word)*

High attains the number five since "index" contains five characters in it. The variable low attains the negative digit of the length of the expression or word which is responsible for assigning a minus symbol ahead of what a number perform. This means that the low will attain the number of -5. This would stand for the range from which we need to grasp a random value. Our main intention was to create a random value between, and incorporating, -5 up to, but not incorporating, 5. What we have just illustrated is the way the *random.randrange()* function operates. If a person goes through it two arguments, it will result in a random value that is from and incorporating the low concluding point, up to, but not involving, the concluding high point. So in our sample below, that's how the line would like:

position = random.randrange(low, high)
which would result -5, -4, -3, -2, -1, 0, 1, 2, 3, or 4. This is the thing that we needed because these values are all the possible accepted position values for the string "index."

Eventually, we generated a *for loop* that implements ten times. In the loop structure, the project selects a random position number and then prints that position number and correlating letter:

for i in range(10):

print "word[", position, "]\t", word[position]
position = random.randrange(low, high)

Understanding String Immutability

Patterns or Sequences are presented in one of the two categories, which can be either mutable or immutable (we needed to realize that they all more on the computer jargon). Mutable sequence implies that they are changeable. Sequence or pattern which is mutable is one a person can alter. On the other hand, the immutable sequence is that one that is unchangeable. So, a pattern or sequence which is immutable is one that a person cannot alter. Strings are said to be the immutable pattern that implies that they cannot convert. So, for instance, the string "Game Over!" will at all-time be the string "Game Over!" Since a person cannot alter it (In fact, it is argued that no one can alter any string they create). Now, people may think, from their previous interaction with strings, that we are wrong here. They may even run an informative

97

session to confirm that they can alter a string, something that could be close to this:

```
>> name = "Nellys"
>> print name Nelly
>> name = "Molly"
>> print name Molly
```

These people may provide this as evidence that implies that they can alter a string. After all, they converted the string "Nelly" to "Molly." But, they may think that they have changed a string in that sample that they provide, but in the real sense, they have not changed anything. Instead, what they just did is to create two distinct strings. In the first sample, they generated a string "Nelly" and allocated it to the variable identity or name. Then they proceeded in the second sample to develop another string, "Molly" and allocated it to identity. Now, both "Nelly" and "Molly" are perfect identities, but they are distinct names or identities and will always remain like that, just as they are distinct strings and they will always remain like that. Another alternative to handle this is to assume that strings are typed in ink on a sheet of paper. We can cast out a sheet of paper with a string on it and substitute it with another sheet of paper with a brand-new string on it, but we cannot alter the assertion the moment that they have been noted.

Therefore, we may also ponder that this is much fuss about nothing. So what would happen if a string is immutable? But actually, it is noted that immutable strings do have upshot. Because people cannot alter a string, in most cases they cannot allocate a new nature to a string via indexing. Below is an example of an interactive session to illustrate to you what we actually mean:

```
>> word = "game"
>> word[0] = "l"
Traceback (most recent call last): File "<pyshell#1>", line 1, in ?
word[0] = "l"
TypeError: the tool does not support item task
```

In the above-illustrated session, our main desire was to alter the string "game" to the string "lame", which bluntly we did not much like the game we were referring to. All that we wanted to carry out here was to alter the letter "g" to an "l." So we allocated "l" to the initial position in the string, word [0]. But as people can observe, this produced in a big, fat mistake or error that is misinterpret our information. The interpretation would even show us that strings do not aid item task, as people cannot allocate a new number to a character in a string. But, just since people cannot change a string does not imply that they cannot develop new strings from subsisting ones.

Building a New String

We have already observed how a person can concatenate two strings using the + processor. Often we might need to construct a brand-new string, with a single character one after the other. Because strings are immutable, what we would be carrying out is generating a new string each time awe apply them in the concatenation operator.

Initiating the No Vowels Program

This proceeding program, No Vowels, attains a text from the programmer and prints it, minus any vowels. The project develops a new string of the first text or information, without the vowels. It is said that what it does is to generate a series of new strings. Here is an example of how the code looks:

 # No Vowels

 # Illustrates developing new strings with a for loop # Michael Dawson - 1/27/03

message or text= raw_input("Enter a message or text: ") new_message = ""

VOWELS = "aeiou"

print

for a letter in message or text:

if letter.lower() not in VOWELS: new_message += letter

print "A new string has been generated, "new_message or text print "\nYour text or message without vowels is:", new_message raw_input("\n\nPress the enter key to exit.")

Developing Constants

After the program attains the message or text from the Programmer and develops an empty new text, it generates a string:

VOWELS = "aeiou"

This mutable, VOWELS, is allotted to a string of all the vowels. A person may presumably realize that the variable identify is in all caps, opposite to what he or she have learned: that would imply to a traditional variable identity that is in lowercase. Well, we have not swerved from tradition here; there is a special implication that is related to the variable identity in all caps.

They are known as constants and refers to a digit, number, or value that is not purposed to alter (their value is constant). Constants are essential to the users in two means. Using the mutable name rather than the string is explicit. The moment a person perceives the variable identity, he or she understand what it implies to, but he or she may also be perplexed by observing the odd-looking string itself. Secondly,

100

constants have a role in saving rewriting and more possibly mistakes from miswriting. Constants are specifically essential if a person has an extended value, like a much-extended value or string. People can apply a constant in a project where he or she has the same, unchanging numbers involved in many places.

Developing New Strings from Subsisting Ones

The actual task of the project takes place in the loop. The program develops a new text or message, without any vowels, as the loop operates. Every moment via the PC examines the proceeding letter in the original text or message. If it is not a vowel, it appends this letter to the new text it is introducing. If it is a vowel, the project goes to the following letter. A person may realize that a program cannot attach a nature to a string, so, more exactly, the moment the program meets a character that is not a vowel, it concatenates the brand-new information it has so far with this character or feature. The code that completes this may look like is:

```
for a letter in message or text:
if letter.lower() not in VOWELS: new_message or text += letter
print "A brand-new string has been generated:", new_message or text
```

There are two distinct brand-new concepts in the loop, so allow me to illustrate both of them to you for you to understand them. First, Python is very selective when it comes to dealing with the strings and characters. "A" is distinct from "a". Because the VOWELS is allotted a string that has only lowercase letters, we wanted to ensure that we checked only the lowercase letters the moment we are applying the in processor or operator. That is why we applied *letter.lower()*. Second, a person may also realize that we applied the augmented task processor,

+=, in the project for string concatenation. We also able to illustrate the augmented task processor with values, but they also run with strings. This is illustrated below:

new_message += letter
is literally the same as
new_message = new_message + letter

Slicing Strings

Indexing is an essential strategy, but people would not be constrained to duplicating just a single unit at a time from a pattern. They can always create copies of continuous segments of units known as the slices. They may also copy or slice a single unit element like indexing or section of a sequence or pattern like the middle three units. Finally, people can also develop a slice that is a duplicate of the entire sequence or pattern. So, for strings, that would imply that people may grasp anything between a one characters, to a team of successive characters, to all string.

Initiating the Pizza Slicer Program

The Pizza Slicer project allows a person to slice the string "pizza" any means he or she wants. It is a perfect interactive means to aid a person to understand slicing. All he or she needs to do is enter the beginning and concluding positions of the slice, and the project exhibits the outcome. Here is an example of how the code would look like:

```
# Pizza Slicer
# Illustrates string slicing # Michael Dawson - 1/27/03
word = "pizza" print \
"""
```

102

Slicing 'Cheat Sheet'

```
0   1      2       3       4       5
+—--+—--+—--+—--+—--+
|  p  |    i    |    z    |    z    |  a  |
+—-+—-+—-+—-+—-+
-5  -4      -3      -2      -1
"""
```

print "Enter the starting and concluding index for a person's slice of 'pizza'." print "Click the enter button at 'Start' to exit."
begin = None
while begin != "":
begin = (raw_input("\nBegin: "))

if begin:

begin = int(begin)
end = int(raw_input("End: "))
print "word[", begin, ":", end, "]\t\t", print word[begin:end]
raw_input("\n\nClick the enter button to exit.")

Initiating None

Before a person reaches the code concerning slicing, he or she needs to have a look at the line that introduces a new concept: *begin = None*. The line allocates a unique value, known as None, to start or begin. None is usually the Python's system of representing nothing. None creates a perfect placeholder for a number or value. It also assesses to false the moment it is treated as a condition. It has been applied here since we needed to introduce begin for use in the *while loop* condition.

Understanding Slicing

Generating a slice is the same as to indexing. But rather than utilizing one position number, a person may supply a beginning and concluding position. Each component between the two positions becomes a segment of the slice, to itemize the concluding points of a slice, incorporating both in parenthesis, isolated by a colon. Here is a quick sample of the interactive session to illustrate what we mean:

```
>> word = "pizza"
>> print word[0:6] pizza
>> print word[1:4] iz
>> print word[-4:-2] iz
>> print word[-4:3] iz
```

Word [0:6] gets back to the whole string since all its characters are between those two concluding positions. Word [1:4] gets back the string "iz" since those two natures are between the concluding positions. Similar to indexing, a person may apply negative digits. Word [-4:-2] also provides the string "iz" since those natures are between the two negative points. Individuals may also mix and tie positive and negative concluding positions. This function like developing any other slice; the components between the two points values will be in the slice. So, word[-4:3] also offers the string "iz", since they are the two natures between those two concluding positions.

The trap here will apply If a person develops an "impossible" slice, where the beginning position which is much massive than the ending point, like word[2:1], a person may not make an error. Rather, Python will quietly get back a negative pattern or sequence. For strings, that implies a person will attain the empty string. So he or she needs to be careful since this is presumably not the sort of result they are after.

Developing Slices

In the interior of the loop of the program Pizza Slicer, the program will prints the syntax for developing a slice structured on the starting and concluding positions the programmer entered, via the proceeding line bellow:

print "word[", begin, ":", end, "]\t\t",
Then, the project prints the real slice applying the variables begin and end: print word[begin: end]

Applying Slicing Shorthand

Although a person may attain each possible slice by particularizing on two values, there are some slicing shortcuts a person may apply. A person may exclude the starting position for the slice to begin the slice at the starting or beginning of the pattern or sequence. So, provided that word has been allotted "pizza", the slice word[:5] is actually similar to the word[0:3]. A person may exclude the concluding position so that the slice concludes with the very final unit or element. So, word[2:] is a shorthand for the word[2:5]. That person can also leave out both values to reach a slice that is the whole pattern. So, word[:] is simply a shorthand for the word[0:5]. Below is a sample of an interactive session to support this proposition:

>> word = "pizza"
>> word[0:3] 'pizz'
>> word[:5] 'pizz'
>> word[2:5] 'zza'
>> word[2:] 'zza'
>> word[0:5] 'pizza'
>> word[:] 'pizza'

Creating Tuples

Tuples refer to a form of a pattern, like strings. But unlike strings, which only have certain characters, tuples have components of any form. That implies that a person may contain a tuple that keeps a bunch of great scores for a game, or one that stores a team of workers names. But tuple components do not contain to all be of the similar model. A person might generate a tuple having both strings and digits if he or she or she needed, while he or she does not have to end a string and values. That person may develop a tuple that has a pattern of graphic pictures, sound documents, or even a team of aliens, the moment he or she comes to know how to develop these things, which we shall study later in this chapter. Whatever a person may allot to a variable, he or she can team together and keep them as a pattern in a tuple.

Initiating the Hero's Inventory Program

Hero's Inventory keeps the inventory of a paladin from a basic role-playing game. Similar to most of the role-playing games ever generated, the paladin is from a minimal, trifling village. His male parent, of course, murdered by an evil warlord, the question here is; would there be a pursuit without a dead father? And now that the paladin has come of age, is it the moment to take his revenge? In this project, the paladin's statement or inventory is stood for by a tuple. The tuple has strings, one for every object in the paladin's occupation. The hero begins out with nothing but then proceeds to provide some items. The following code illustrates the humble starting of our hero's drive. Here is how the code for the program looks like:

```
# Paladin's Inventory
# Illustrates tuple generation # Michael Dawson - 1/29/03
```

```
# develop an empty tuple inventory = ()
# treat the tuple as a condition if not inventory:
print "You are empty-handed."
raw_input("\nClick the enter button to continue.")
# develop a tuple with some objects inventory = ("sword",
"armor",
"shield", "healing potion")
# print the tuple
print "\nThe tuple inventory is:\n", inventory
# print every component in the tuple print "\nYour items:"
for the item in inventory: print object
raw_input("\n\nClick the enter button to exit.")
```

Developing an Empty Tuple

To developing a tuple, a person needs to encircle a list of numbers, isolated by commas, with the brackets. Even a set of lone bracket or parentheses is an accepted but empty tuple. We developed an empty tuple in the first section of the project to illustrate that the hero contains nothing: *inventory = ()*. It is as easy as that. So in this line, the mutable inventory obtains an empty tuple.

Treating a Tuple as a Condition

The moment we discussed conditions, we were able to point out that people can treat any digit in Python as a condition. That implies that a person may address a tuple as a state, too. And that is what we did in the proceeding lines:

```
if not inventory:
print "You are empty-handed."
```

107

As a state, a desolate tuple is false or wrong. A tuple with at least a single component is accurate. Because the tuple allocated to inventory is empty, it is inaccurate or erroneous. That would imply that no inventory is actual. So the PC prints the string, "A person is empty-handed.", just as it should.

Developed a Tuple with Components

A defenseless paladin is a tedious hero. So next, we generated a new tuple with string component that stands for essential objects for our paladin. We allotted this new tuple to inventory with the following:

```
inventory = ("sword",
"armor",
"shield",
"healing potion")
```

A comma isolates every component in the tuple. That creates the first component the string "sword", the proceeds "armor", then proceed "shield", and the final component "healing point". So every string is one component in this tuple. Besides, realize that the tuple spans many lines. A person may type a tuple in a single line, or span it across various lines like we did provide that he or she concludes every line after a comma. These cases are always sporadic and this one of the few instances where Python allows individuals to break up an assertion across many lines.

Printing a Tuple

Though a tuple may also have multiple components, a person may print the whole tuple just like we can with any single digit. That is what has been done in the following line: *print "\nThe tuple inventory* *is:\n", inventory.* The PC exhibits all of the components, encircled by brackets.

Looping Via a Tuple's Components

Eventually, we typed a *for loop* to go inline via the units in inventory and print every single individually:

> *print "\nYour items:" for an object in inventory:*
> *print item*

This loop writes every component or every string in inventory on a distinct line. This loop appears just like the ones a person have seen with strings. Indeed a person may apply this type of circuit to run via the components of any pattern. Even though it developed a tuple where all the components are of a similar category, strings in this case, tuples do not contain to be filled with numbers of a similar class. A single tuple may as have integers, lines, and floating-point digits, for instance.

Using Tuples

Because tuples are uncomplicated another type sequence that everything a person studied concerning patterns from strings toils with tuples. A person may attain the span of a tuple, print every unit with a for loop, and apply in the processor to measure if a group in a tuple. A person can also index, slice, and concatenate tuples, at the same time too.

Initiating the Hero's Inventory 2.0

Our paladin's drive keeps. In this project, tested, his inventory is computed, and sliced. Our paladin will also take place upon a chest with objects in it. Via the tuple concatenation, our paladin's or hero's inventory will be substituted with all of his current objects plus the cherish he finds in the chest. Because this project is a bit extended, we will actually run through the code in a single part at a time instead of illustrating a person the entire thing at the moment.

Setting Up the Program

The initial section of the project functions like it did in the earlier project, Hero's Inventory. These strings develop a tuple and print out every unit:

```
# Hero's Inventory 2.0
# Illustrates tuples
# Michael Dawson - 1/29/03
# develop a tuple with some objects and exhibit with a for loop inventory
= ("sword",
"armor",
"shield", "healing potion")
print "Your objects:" for objects in inventory:
print object
raw_input("\nClick the enter button to continue.")
```

Appling the len() Function with Tuples

The len() function operates with tuples the way it operates with strings. If people need to know the span of a tuple, they then need to put it inside the parentheses. The function gets back the digit of the component in the tuple. Desolate tuples, or any other desolate patterns for that matter, have a span of 0. The next strings apply the len() function with the tuple:

```
# get the length a tuple
```

> *print "You have", len(inventory), "objects in your possession."*
> *raw_input("\nClick the enter button to proceed.")*

Because this tuple contains four units including the four strings, "sword," "armor," "shield," and "healing potion," the text a person may have is four objects in their possession, which is displayed.

The trap here would involve a person to realize that in the tuple inventory, the string "healing potion" is computed as one unit, even though it is compost of two words. One string is usually regarded as a single unit in a tuple since it does not matter the number of individual words present in it.

Applying the in Processor with Tuples

Just like a person uses strings, he or she may also apply them *in the processor* with tuples to evaluate for component membership. And, just like the first time, the *in the processor* is always used to develop a condition. That is the way it has also been applied in the following examples:

> *# trail for membership within*
> *if "healing potion" in inventory:*
> *l always live to fight another day."*

The state "healing potion" in inventory trail if the whole string "healing potion" is a component in inventory. Because it is, the information people will live to fight another day, which is displayed.

Indexing Tuples

Indexing tuples toils in the same way indexing strings works. A person is required to specify a point digit, in parenthesis, to ingress a certain component. In the proceeding strings, we have allowed the programmer to opt the index digit and then the PC to displays the correlating with the components:

 # display a single object via an index
index = int(raw_input("\nEnter the index value for an object in inventory: ")) print "At index", index, "is", inventory[index]

Slicing Tuples

A person may provide a starting and concluding position when e/she slice the functions similarly with strings, just as it was illustrated before. The result is a tuple having each component between those two positions. Just as we saw the Pizza Slicer project from the previous chapter, we allowed the programmer to select the starting and concluding point numbers. Then, just like previously, the program exhibits the slice:

 # display a slice
begin = int(raw_input("\nEnter the index value to start a slice: ")) end = int(raw_input("Enter the index value to conclude the slice: ")) print "inventory[", begin, ":", end, "]\t\t",
print inventory[begin:end]
raw_input("\nClick the enter button to proceed.")

Understanding Tuple Immutability

Tuples are immutable just like strings. That would imply that a person cannot be able to alter them. The following is an interactive session to confirm my argument:

>> inventory = ("shield", "sword", "healing potion", "armor")
>> print inventory

("shield", "sword", "healing potion", "armor")
>>> inventory[0] = "battleax" Traceback (most current call last):
File "<pyshell#3>", line 1, in ? inventory[0] = "battleax"

Concatenating Tuples

A person can concatenate tuples similar to the way he or she can concatenate strings. What he or she needs to do is to attach or join them together with +, the concatenation processor or operator:

```
# concatenate two tuples chest = ("gold", "gems")
Print "A person may find a chest. This has:" print chest
print "Then he or she appends the contents of the chest to his or her
inventory." inventory += chest
print "His or her inventory is now:" print inventory
raw_input("\n\nClick the enter button to exit.")
```

The first activity that we carried out here was to develop a brand-new tuple, chest, which contained the two string components, "gold" and "gems." Then we proceeded to the printed chest to illustrate its key components. After that, we applied an augmented task operator or processor to concatenate inventory with chest and allot the outcome back to the inventory. We did not redefine the first or initial tuple allotted to inventory, because this would be impossible since tuples are unchangeable. Rather, the augmented task processor developed a new tuple containing the components from inventory and chest and allots that to the inventory.

Back to the Word Jumble Game

The Word Jumble game fuses various brand-new concepts that we have discussed and analyzed before in this chapter. A person may simply change the program to have his or her list of assertions to guess.

Setting Up the Program

After our fist comments, we were able to ship in the random module:

 # Word Jumble #

 # The PC selects a random assertion and then "jumbles" it

 # The player has to guess the initial word

#

 # Michael Dawson - 1/28/03 ship in random

The proceeding task we were able to carry out was to apply a tuple to develop a pattern of statements. If perhaps you follow this closely, you will realize that variable name or identity WORD is in typed or written caps, meaning that we can treat it as a constant as follow:

 # develop a pattern or sequence of words to opt from

WORDS = ("python", "jumble", "simple", "hard", "response", "xylophone")

Next, we applied a brand-new function known as, *random.choice(),* to grasp random word from WORDS: # pick one word randomly from the sequence

word = random.choice(WORDS)

This function is probably new to people, but it also quite easy to understand. The PC looks for whatever pattern a person gives and selects a random component. The moment the PC has opted for a random word, it allocates it to a word. This is the exact word that the player will have to guess. Finally, we mapped the word to accurate, which we will be applying later to observe if the player makes a precise guess: *# develop a variable to apply then to find if the belief is the right = word*

Planning the Jumble Development Section

The following section of code applies the brand-new ideas in the chapter, and indeed, it is the most surprising section of the program. It is the part that generates the jumbled word from the initial, randomly opted word. But, before we type any code, we designed out this section of the project in the pseudocode (yes, where we applied all that stuff we typed about). Below is the first pass at the algorithm to develop a jumbled word from the opted word:

form a desolate jumble word
while the opted statement contain letters in it
extract a random letter from the opted
a statement that is attached to the
random letter to the jumbled word

Conceptually, this is quite perfect, but we have to observe our semantics first. Since strings are unchangeable, we cannot really "extricate a random letter" from the string that the programmer entered. But, we can instead develop a brand new string that does not have the randomly opted letter. And while we cannot "append the random letter" to the jumble statement string either, we can opt to develop a new string by concatenating the recent jumble assertion with the "extricated" letter.

Developing an Empty Jumble String

The very original section of the algorithm is pretty simple: # *develop a jumbled model of the word jumble =""*

The program prepares the desolate string and allocates it to jumble, which then cites it back to the last jumbled word.

Setting Up the Loop

A while loop manages the jumble development operation. The loop state is quite natural, as a person may perceive this: *while word:*

We positioned the loop up in this position to enable it to proceed until a word is equivalent to the empty string. This is good, since every moment the loop implements, the PC always develop a brand-new model of Scripture with a single letter "extricated" and allocates it back to the original word. Finally, word will get the desolate string, and the jumbling will be completed after that.

Creating a Random Position in word

The opening line in the loop structure develops a random position in the world, rooted in its length:

$$position = random.randrange(len(word))$$

This would imply that the letter word[position] is the letter that would be "extricated" from word and "attached to" the word jumble.

Developing a New Model of a jumble

The proceeding string in the loop develops a brand-new model of the string jumble. Which then probably equivalent to its old self, with the letter word[position]. And the jumble += word[position]

Developing a New Model of word

The proceeding string in the loop, word = word[: position] + word[(position + 1):] develops a brand-new mode of a statement without the single letter at the position. Applying to slice will aid the PC to develop two brand-new strings from the word. The initial slice, word[: position], is each letter up to, but not incorporating, word[position]. The following slice, word[(position + 1):], is each letter after word[position]. These two string are connected and allotted to a statement or word, that is at the moment equivalent to its old self, without the single-letter word[position].

Welcoming the Player

After the jumbled statement has been developed, the proceeding part of the program invites or welcomes the player to the game and exhibits the jumbled assertion to be reorganized:

> *# begin the game print *
> *"""*
> *Welcome to Word Jumble!*
> *You need to unscramble the letters to construct a word. (Click the enter button at the prompt to exit or quit.) """*
> *print "The jumble is:," jumble*

Getting the Player's Guess

Next, the PC receives the player's guess. The PC continues to ask the player for a guess provided that the player does not enter the accurate word or pushes the Enter button at the prompt:

> *guess = raw_input("\n A person's guess: ") guess = guess.lower()*
> *while (guess != accurate) and (guess != ""): print "Sorry, that's not it."*
> *guess = raw_input("A person's guess: ") guess = guess.lower()*

We have to make sure that we alter the guess to lowercase because the word the player is attempting to guess is in lowercase.

Congratulating the Player

At this point, the player could have either guessed the statement accurately or exit the game in the program. In the case where he or she has guessed the word accurately, the PC will give him a congratulation message on the screen o his or her PC:

if guess == right:
Print "That's it! You guessed it! \n"

Concluding the Game

Eventually, the program thanks or appreciates the player for frolicking the game and concludes:

print "Thanks for playing." raw_input("\n\nClick the enter button to exit.")

Chapter Five

Lists and Dictionaries: The Hangman Game

Tuples are the preferred means in which we can work with the pattern of any form; the only thing that can be limiting with them is their immutability. Luckily, another pattern type referred to like lists, carries out all that that tuples can do, plus many other things. That is since lists are changeable. Units may be appended or deleted from a list. We then may sort or back-pedal the whole list. We may also be initiated to another model, dictionaries. While lists operate with pattern message or information, dictionaries operate with sets of data. Dictionaries, allows us to look upon a single number with another, just like their fellow lists. In this chapter, we shall specify the following:

- How to develop, index, and slice a list

- How we can add and remove or delete units from a list

- How we can apply list strategies to add, sort, and back-pedal or reverse a list

- We shall also learn how we can apply nested patterns or sequences to represent more sophisticated information or data

- We shall also discuss dictionaries to and how it functions with sets of data or information

- We will learn how to append and remove dictionary objects

119

Initiating the Hangman Game

The program for this topic and chapter will be about the game of hangman. The PC selects a secret word, and the player contains to attempt to guess it, a single letter at a time. Every moment the player makes a false guess, the PC illustrates a brand-new image of a figure being portrayed. If the player does not guess the statement in time, the stick integer is a goner.

Using Lists

Lists are referred to as patterns; lists are also mutable just like tuples. They may be redesigned. So, lists can perform everything tuples can, plus many other things. They function in the same way like tuples; this implies that everything we are going to discuss here is going to be about tuples and how they used to lists, which prompt learning to apply them as a snap.

Initiating the Hero's Inventory 3.0 Program

This project is rooted in the Hero's Inventory 2.0 program, which was launched earlier in chapter 4 of this book, the part "Developing Tuples" but rather than applying tuples to keep the hero's inventory, where this project involves lists. The initial section of the Hero's Inventory 3.0 develops a similar outcome as Model or version 2.0. The code is almost the same; the only distinction that is present is that systems use lists rather than tuples. The next section of the project e second part of the program takes merits of the changeability of lists and performs some new tasks with the patterns.

Developing a List

The initial string of the project develops a brand-new list, allocates it to inventory, and prints every component. The final string waits for the programmer before proceeding. This functions almost in the same way as it did in Hero's Inventory 2.0. The only distinction that presents itself is that we encircled the components with square brackets rather than of parentheses, to generate a list rather than a tuple.

```
# Hero's Inventory
# Illustrates lists
# Michael Dawson - 1/29/03
# develop a list with some objects and exhibit with a for loop inventory =
["sword", "armor", "shield", "healing potion"] print "Your objects:"
for objects in inventory: print objects
raw_input("\nClick the enter button to proceed.")
```

Applying the len() Function with Lists

The proceeding code is exactly similar to the correlating code in Hero's Inventory 2.0:

```
# attain the length of a list
print "A person has," len(inventory), "objects in their possession.
" raw_input("\nPClick the enter button to proceed.")
```

Applying the in Processor with Lists

Once more, the code for this part is similar to those in the older model. The *in processor* functions in the same manner with lists as it performs with tuples.

```
# trial for membership within
if "healing potion" in inventory:
print "A Person will live to fight another day."
```

121

Indexing Lists

Here, the code is similar as it was with tuples. Indexing a list is similar to indexing a tuple: you need to distribute the position digit of the component that you are after in the parentheses.

```
# display a single object via an index
index = int(raw_input("\nEnter the index digit for an object in inventory: "))
print "At index", index, "is", inventory[index]
```

Slicing Lists

Would a person hold slicing a list is similar as slicing a tuple? Once more, a person may distribute the two concluding points, isolated by a colon, in parenthesizes:

```
# display a slice
Start= int(raw_input("\nEnter the index digit to start a slice: "))
Concluding point= int(raw_input("Enter the index digit to conclude the slice: "))
print "inventory[", start, ":", conclude, "]\t\t",
print inventory[begin:end]
raw_input("\nClick the enter button to proceed.")
```

Concatenating Lists

Concatenating lists functions in a similar way as concatenating tuples functions. The only distinction that comes in here is that we developed a list instead of a tuple and allocated it to the chest. This difference might seem minimal but it is very crucial, since a person may only concatenate patterns of the same category.

```
# concatenate two lists chest = ["gold", "gems"]
```

print "A person find a chest which has:" print chest

print "A person appends the contents of the chest to his or her inventory."

inventory += chest

print "A person inventory is now:" print inventory

raw_input("\nClick the enter button to proceed.")

Understanding List Mutability

At this position a person can be getting a bit exhausted of reading the phrase "operates in a similar way as tuples." Up to this juncture, with the exception of applying brackets rather than parentheses, lists appear to have no distinction than tuples. But there is a single large distinction between them. Lists are mutable; this would imply that they may be altered. This results in lists being robust and pliable pattern form at a person's disposal. Because lists are changeable, there are various things a person may perform with them that person cannot perform with tuples.

Assigning a New List Component by Index

Since lists are changeable, a person may allot a subsisting component a brand-new value:

```
#allot by index
print "A person's trade his or her sword for a crossbow."
inventory[0] = "crossbow"
print "A person's inventory is now:" print inventory
raw_input("\nClick the enter button to proceed.")
```

The next string allots the string "crossbow" to the component in inventory at point 0: inventory[0] = "crossbow." The brand-new string substitutes the earlier value, which was "sword." A person may perceive the outcome the moment the print statement exhibits the brand-new model of inventory.

Assigning a New List Slice

Besides assigning a brand-new number to one component, a person may allot a brand-new number to a slice. We allocated the list ["orb of upcoming telling"] to the slice inventory[4:6]:

```
# allot by slice
print "A person applies his or her gold and gems to purchase an orb of upcoming telling.
" inventory[4:6] = ["orb of upcoming telling"]
print "A person's inventory is now:" print inventory
raw_input("\nClick the enter button to proceed.")
```

This task assertion substitutes the two objects inventory [4] and inventory[5] using the string "orb of upcoming telling." Since we allocated a list with a single component to a slice with two components, the span of the list is said to have shrunk by one.

Conclusion

Congratulations for completing the book! Although there are plenty of samples to play around with throughout the book, these programs are just scratching the surface and really are meant to give you a feel of how flexible Python is and how far you can take a bunch of seemingly basic commands and concepts. Your next step would be to tweak these programs and get them to do other things and keep coding and practicing to get them to evolve to more sophisticated programs. Python is not very hard to learn and mastering the basics really help make the advanced concepts easier to grasp thus making web apps, games, mods, scripts and other programs far more fun! Good luck!

www.ingramcontent.com/pod-product-compliance
Lightning Source LLC
LaVergne TN
LVHW051246050326
832903LV00028B/2600